STATUS ANXIETY

STATUS ANXIETY

Alain de Botton

Pantheon Books, New York

Pantheon Books and colophon are registered trademarks of Random House, Inc.

Grateful acknowledgment is made to HarperCollins Publishers, Inc. for permission to reprint
an excerpt from "Something for the Touts, the Nuns, the Grocery Clerks and You" from
Burning in Water, Drowning in Flame: Selected Poems 1955–1973 by Charles Bukowski.
Copyright © 1963, 1964, 1965, 1966, 1967, 1968, 1974 by Charles Bukowski.
Reprinted by permission of HarperCollins Publishers, Inc.

Library of Congress Cataloging-in-Publication Data

De Botton, Alain.
Status anxiety / Alain de Botton.
p. cm.
ISBN 0-375-42083-5
1. Social status. 2. Social status—Psychological aspects. I. Title.
HM821.D43 2003
305—dc22   2003061018

www.pantheonbooks.com

Book design by Austin Taylor

Printed in the United States of America

First Edition

2 4 6 8 9 7 5 3 1

CONTENTS

DEFINITIONS

Status

— One's position in society; the word derived from the Latin *statum* or standing (past participle of the verb *stare,* to stand).

— In a narrow sense, the word refers to one's legal or professional standing within a group (married, a lieutenant, etc.). But in the broader—and here more relevant—sense, to one's value and importance in the eyes of the world.

— Different societies have awarded status to different groups: hunters, fighters, ancient families, priests, knights, fecund women. Increasingly since 1776, status in the West (the vague but comprehensible territory here under discussion) has been awarded in relation to financial achievement.

— The consequences of high status are pleasant. They include resources, freedom, space, comfort, time and, as importantly perhaps, a sense of being cared for and thought valuable—conveyed through invitations, flattery, laughter (even when the joke lacked bite), deference and attention.

— High status is thought by many (but freely admitted by few) to be one of the finest of earthly goods.

Status Anxiety

— A worry, so pernicious as to be capable of ruining extended stretches of our lives, that we are in danger of failing to conform to the ideals of success laid down by our society and that we may as a result be stripped of dignity and respect; a worry that we are currently occupying too modest a rung or are about to fall to a lower one.

— The anxiety is provoked by, among other elements, recession, redundancy, promotions, retirement, conversations with colleagues in the same industry, newspaper profiles of the prominent and the greater success of friends. Like confessing to envy (to which the emotion is related), it can be socially imprudent to reveal the extent of any anxiety and, therefore, evidence of the inner drama is uncommon, limited usually to a preoccupied gaze, a brittle smile or an over-extended pause after news of another's achievement.

— If our position on the ladder is a matter of such concern, it is because our self-conception is so dependent upon what others make of us. Rare individuals aside (Socrates, Jesus), we rely on signs of respect from the world to feel tolerable to ourselves.

— More regrettably still, status is hard to achieve and even harder to maintain over a lifetime. Except in societies where it is fixed at birth and our veins flow with noble blood, our position hangs on what we can achieve; and we may fail due to stupidity or an absence of self-knowledge, macro-economics or malevolence.

— And from failure will flow humiliation: a corroding awareness that we have been unable to convince the world of our value and are henceforth condemned to consider the successful with bitterness and ourselves with shame.

Thesis

— That status anxiety possesses an exceptional capacity to inspire sorrow.

— That the hunger for status, like all appetites, can have its uses: spurring us to do justice to our talents, encouraging excellence, restraining us from harmful eccentricities and cementing members of a society around a common value system. But, like all appetites, its excesses can also kill.

— That the most profitable way of addressing the condition may be to attempt to understand and to speak of it.

PART ONE

CAUSES

I

LOVELESSNESS

Our Need for Love, Our Desire for Status

1.

Every adult life could be said to be defined by two great love stories. The first—the story of our quest for sexual love—is well known and well charted, its vagaries form the staple of music and literature, it is socially accepted and celebrated. The second—the story of our quest for love from the world—is a more secret and shameful tale. If mentioned, it tends to be in caustic, mocking terms, as something of interest chiefly to envious or deficient souls, or else the drive for status is interpreted in an economic sense alone. And yet this second love story is no less intense than the first, it is no less complicated, important or universal, and its setbacks are no less painful. There is heartbreak here too.

2.

Adam Smith, *The Theory of Moral Sentiments* (Edinburgh, 1759):
"To what purpose is all the toil and bustle of this world? What is the end of avarice and ambition, of the pursuit of wealth, of power and pre-eminence? Is it to supply the necessities of nature? The wages of the meanest labourer can supply them. What then are the advantages of that great purpose of human life which we call *bettering our condition*?

"To be observed, to be attended to, to be taken notice of with sympathy, complacency, and approbation, are all the advantages which we can propose to derive from it. The rich man glories in his riches because he feels that they naturally draw upon him the attention of the world. The poor man on the contrary is ashamed of his poverty.

He feels that it places him out of the sight of mankind. To feel that we are taken no notice of necessarily disappoints the most ardent desires of human nature. The poor man goes out and comes in unheeded, and when in the midst of a crowd is in the same obscurity as if shut up in his own hovel. The man of rank and distinction, on the contrary, is observed by all the world. Everybody is eager to look at him. His actions are the objects of the public care. Scarce a word, scarce a gesture that fall from him will be neglected."

3.

The predominant impulse behind our desire to rise in the social hierarchy may be rooted not so much in the material goods we can accrue or the power we can wield as in the amount of love we stand to receive as a consequence of high status. Money, fame and influence may be valued more as tokens of—and means to—love rather than ends in themselves.

How may a word, generally used only in relation to what we would expect or hope for from a parent, or a romantic partner, be applied to something we might want from and be offered by the world? Perhaps we can define love, at once in its familial, sexual and worldly forms, as a kind of respect, a sensitivity on the part of one person to another's existence. To be shown love is to feel ourselves the object of concern: our presence is noted, our name is registered, our views are listened to, our failings are treated with indulgence and our needs are ministered to. And under such care, we flourish. There may be differences between romantic and status forms of love—the latter has no sexual dimension, it cannot end in marriage, those who offer it usually bear secondary motives—and yet status beloveds will, just like romantic ones, enjoy protection under the benevolent gaze of appreciative others.

People who hold important positions in society are commonly labelled "somebodies," and their inverse "nobodies"—both of which are, of course, nonsensical descriptors, for we are all, by necessity, individuals with distinct identities and comparable claims on existence. Such words are nevertheless an apt vehicle for conveying the disparate treatment accorded to different groups. Those without status are all but invisible: they are treated brusquely by others, their complexities trampled upon and their singularities ignored.

While there will inevitably be economic ramifications, the impact of low status should not be read in material terms alone. The gravest penalty rarely lies—above subsistence levels, at least—in mere physical discomfort; it consists more often, even primarily, in the challenge that low status poses to a person's sense of self-respect. Provided that it is not accompanied by humiliation, discomfort can be endured for long periods without complaint. For proof of this, we have only to look to the example of the many soldiers and explorers who have, over the centuries, willingly tolerated privations far exceeding those suffered by the poorest members of their societies, so long as they were sustained throughout their hardships by an awareness of the esteem in which they were held by others.

The benefits of high status are similarly seldom limited to wealth. We should not be surprised to find many of the already affluent continuing to accumulate sums beyond anything that five generations might spend. Their endeavours are peculiar only if we insist on a strictly material rationale behind wealth creation. As much as money, they seek the respect that stands to be derived from the process of gathering it. Few of us are determined aesthetes or sybarites, yet almost all of us hunger for dignity; and if a future society were to offer love as a reward for accumulating small plastic discs, then it would not be long before such worthless items too assumed a central place in our most zealous aspirations and anxieties.

4.

William James, *The Principles of Psychology* (Boston, 1890):
"No more fiendish punishment could be devised, were such a thing physically possible, than that one should be turned loose in society and remain absolutely unnoticed by all the members thereof. If no one turned around when we entered, answered when we spoke, or minded what we did, but if every person we met 'cut us dead,' and acted as if we were non-existent things, a kind of rage and impotent despair would before long well up in us, from which the cruellest bodily torture would be a relief."

5.

How are we affected by an absence of love? Why should being ignored drive us to a "rage and impotent despair" besides which torture itself would be a relief?

The attentions of others matter to us because we are afflicted by a congenital uncertainty as to our own value, as a result of which affliction we tend to allow others' appraisals to play a determining role in how we see ourselves. Our sense of identity is held captive by the judgements of those we live among. If they are amused by our jokes, we grow confident in our power to amuse. If they praise us, we develop an impression of high merit. And if they avoid our gaze when we enter a room or look impatient after we have revealed our occupation, we may fall into feelings of self-doubt and worthlessness.

In an ideal world, we would be more impermeable. We would be unshaken whether we were ignored or noticed, admired or ridiculed. If someone praised us insincerely, we would not be unduly seduced. And if we had carried out a fair assessment of our strengths and decided upon our value, another's suggestion that we were inconsequential would not wound us. We would know our worth. Instead, we each appear to hold within ourselves a range of divergent views as to our native qualities. We discern evidence of both cleverness and stupidity, humour and dullness, importance and superfluity. And amid such uncertainty, we typically turn to the wider world to settle the question of our significance. Neglect highlights our latent negative self-assessments, while a smile or compliment as rapidly brings out the converse. We seem beholden to the affections of others to endure ourselves.

Our "ego" or self-conception could be pictured as a leaking balloon, forever requiring the helium of external love to remain inflated, and ever vulnerable to the smallest pinpricks of neglect. There is something at once sobering and absurd in the extent to which we are lifted by the attentions of others and sunk by their disregard. Our mood may blacken because a colleague greets us distractedly or our telephone calls go unreturned. And we are capable of thinking life worth living because someone remembers our name or sends us a fruit basket.

The Consequences of Neglect

OTHERS' ATTITUDE	SELF-IMAGE
You are a failure	I am a disgrace
You are unimportant	I am a nobody
You are dim	I am stupid
	I am worthy
	I am significant
	I am intelligent

The Consequences of Love

OTHERS' ATTITUDE	SELF-IMAGE
You are successful	I am worthy
You are important	I am significant
You are bright	I am intelligent
	I am a disgrace
	I am a nobody
	I am stupid

6.

Given the precariousness of our self-image, it should not be surprising that, from an emotional point of view no less than from a material one, we are anxious about the place we occupy in the world. This place will determine how much love we are offered and so, in turn, whether we can like or must lose confidence in ourselves. It holds the key to a commodity of unprecedented importance to us: a love without which we will be unable to trust or abide by our own characters.

II

EXPECTATION

Nikita Khrushchev and Richard Nixon outside the kitchen of the "Taj Mahal,"
at the American National Exhibition, Moscow, 1959

Material Progress

1.

In July 1959, the American vice president, Richard Nixon, travelled to Moscow to open an exhibition showcasing some of his country's technological and material achievements. The highlight of the exhibition was a full-scale replica of the home of an average member of America's working class, equipped with fitted carpets, a television in the living room, two en suite bathrooms, central heating and a kitchen with a washing machine, a tumble dryer and a refrigerator.

Reporting on this display, an incensed Soviet press angrily denied that an ordinary American worker could conceivably live in such luxury, and advised its readers to dismiss the entire house as propaganda after mockingly baptising it the "Taj Mahal."

When Nixon led Nikita Khrushchev around the exhibition, the leader was comparably sceptical. Outside the kitchen of the model home, Khrushchev pointed to an electric lemon squeezer and remarked to Nixon that no one in his right mind would wish to acquire such a "silly gadget."

"Anything that makes women work less hard must be useful," suggested Nixon.

"We don't think of women in terms of workers—like you do in the capitalist system," snapped an irate Khrushchev.

Later that same evening, Nixon was invited to appear live on Soviet television, an occasion he used to expound on the advantages of American life. Shrewdly, he did not begin his speech by touting democracy or human rights; instead he spoke of money and material progress. Nixon explained that in just a few hundred years, Western countries had managed, through enterprise and industry, to overcome the poverty and famine that had gripped the world until the middle of the eighteenth century and continued even up to the present day to plague many other nations. Americans had purchased 56 million television sets and 143 million radios, he informed his Soviet listeners, a large number of whom did not have private bathrooms or possess so much as a kettle. The members of the average American family could buy nine new dresses and suits and fourteen new pairs of shoes every year, he noted, and some 31 million families owned their own homes. In the United States, houses could be had in a thousand different architectural styles, most boasting greater square footage than the television studio they were broadcasting from. Sitting next to Nixon, an infuriated Khrushchev clenched his fists and mouthed, "*Nyet! Nyet!*"—adding under his breath, according to one account, "*Ëb' tvoyu babushky*" ("Go fuck your grandmother").

2.

Khrushchev's protestation notwithstanding, Nixon's statistics were accurate. In the two centuries preceding his speech, the countries of the West had witnessed the fastest and most dramatic elevation of living standards in human history.

The majority of the population of medieval and early modern Europe had belonged to the peasant class. Impoverished, undernourished, cold and fearful while alive, they were usually dead—following some further agony—before their fortieth birthday. After a lifetime of work, their most valuable possession might have been a cow, a goat or a pot. Famine was never far off, and disease was rife, among the most common conditions being rickets, ulcers, tuberculosis, leprosy, abscesses, gangrene, tumours and cankers.

3.

Then, in early-eighteenth-century Britain, the great Western transformation began. Thanks to new farming techniques (including crop rotation, scientific stock breeding and land consolidation), yields began to increase sharply. Between 1700 and 1820, Britain's agricultural productivity doubled, releasing capital and manpower that flowed into the cities to be invested in industry and trade. The invention of the steam engine and the cotton power loom modified not only working practices but social expectations. Towns exploded in size. In 1800, only one city in the British Isles, London, could boast a population of more than a hundred thousand; by 1891, twenty-three English cities would make that claim. Goods and services that had formerly been the exclusive preserve of the elite were made available to the masses. Luxuries became decencies, and decencies necessities. Daniel Defoe, travelling around southern England in 1745, noted the proliferation of large new shops with enticing window displays and tempting offerings. Whereas for much of recorded history fashion had remained static for decades at a time, it now became possible to identify specific styles for every passing year (in England in 1753, for example, purple was in vogue for women's gowns; in 1754, it was the turn of white linen with a pink pattern; in 1755, dove grey was the rage).

The nineteenth century expanded on and spread the British consumer revolution. Gigantic department stores opened throughout Europe and America: the Bon Marché and Au Printemps in Paris, Selfridge's and Whiteley's in London, Macy's in New York. All were designed to appeal to the new industrial middle class. At a ribbon-cutting ceremony marking the opening of a twelve-storey Marshall Field's in Chicago in 1902, the manager, Gordon Selfridge, proclaimed, "We have built this great institution for ordinary people, so that it can be their store, their downtown home, their buying

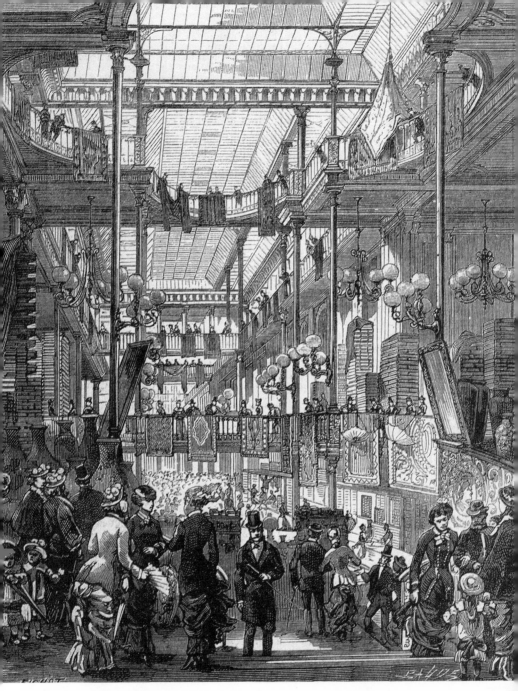

Central staircase, Bon Marché department store, Paris, 1880

headquarters." It was not intended, he emphasised, just for the "swagger rich."

A host of technological inventions helped to stretch mental horizons even as they altered the patterns of everyday life: the old cyclical view of the world, wherein one expected next year to be much like (and just as bad as) last, gave way to the notion that mankind could progress yearly towards perfection. To list only a few of these inventions:

- CORNFLAKES, patented by J. H. Kellogg in 1895 (Kellogg had hit upon the concept by accident, when the grain mixture he served to inmates in his sanatorium unexpectedly hardened and then shattered into flakes)
- the CAN OPENER, patented in 1870
- the SAFETY PIN, invented in 1849
- the SEWING MACHINE, developed by I. M. Singer in 1851 (ready-made clothes would become more common from the 1860s; machine-made underclothes would be introduced in the 1870s)
- the TYPEWRITER, invented in 1867 (the first full-length manuscript to be typed was Mark Twain's *Life on the Mississippi*, published in 1883)
- PROCESSED FOODS: By the 1860s, the British company Crosse & Blackwell was producing twenty-seven thousand gallons of ketchup a year. In the early 1880s, the chemist Alfred Bird came up with an eggless custard powder. Blancmange powder was developed in the 1870s, and jelly crystals in the 1890s.
- LIGHTING: Stearic candles were used from the 1830s, replacing the much shorter-lived tallow-dip candles of old.
- SANITATION: In 1846, Doulton began manufacturing glazed stoneware pipes, which sparked a revolution in metropolitan sewerage. By the late 1870s, public toilets had begun to spring up in

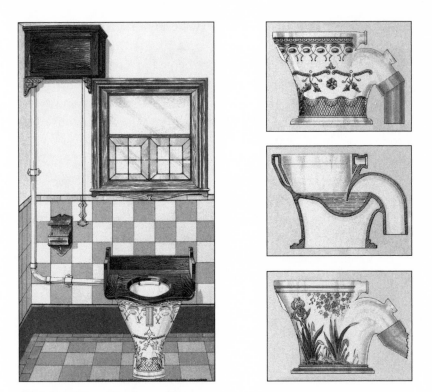

George Jennings, pedestal vase, 1884

Europe and America. George Jennings's famous "pedestal vase" of 1884 stunned the public with its ability to wash away, as its advertisement put it, "ten apples and a flat sponge with a two-gallon flush."

- the TELEPHONE, invented by Alexander Graham Bell in 1875
- DRY CLEANING, invented in 1849 by a Parisian tailor named Jolly-Bellin, who accidentally spilt turpentine on a tablecloth and found that on the patch the spill covered, stains had disappeared (by 1866, Pullars of Perth was offering a postal two-day dry-cleaning service anywhere in the British Isles and had improved

on Jolly-Bellin's cleaning fluid with a formula combining petroleum and benzine).

4.

Material progress accelerated still further in the twentieth century. In his *English Journey* (1934), J. B. Priestley observed that a new England had taken shape, a country of arterial roads and bungalows whose inhabitants, for the most part ordinary workers, read tabloid newspapers, listened to the radio, spent their leisure hours shopping and looked forward to rising incomes year after year. "In this England, for the first time," he asserted, "Jack and Jill are nearly as good as their master and mistress."

George Orwell, in *The Lion and the Unicorn* (1941), sketched a similar picture of the Western material revolution: "Nearly all citizens of civilized countries now enjoy the use of good roads, germ-free water, police protection, free libraries and probably free education of a kind. To an increasing extent the rich and the poor read the same books, and they also see the same films and listen to the same radio programmes. The differences in their way of life have been diminished by the mass-production of cheap clothes and improvements in housing. The place to look for the germs of the future England is in light-industry areas and along the arterial roads. In Slough, Dagenham, Barnet, Letchworth, Hayes—everywhere, indeed, on the outskirts of great towns—the old pattern is gradually changing into something new. In those vast new wildernesses of glass and brick there is a rather restless, culture-less life, centring round tinned food, *Picture Post*, the radio and the internal combustion engine."

When Franklin D. Roosevelt was asked what one book he would give the Soviet people to teach them about the advantages of American society, he singled out the Sears, Roebuck catalogue.

Amid the economic expansion that followed the Second World

The richest woman in the world can have no finer electric cleaner than any woman can have and for as little as 4\frac{50}{}$ *down.* . . . It is The Hoover—one household possession that confers pride of ownership without penalty of cost.

The new and exclusive Hoover Hedlite makes cleaning easy in darkest corners.

Of no other cleaner can this be said: More homes—mansions or cottages—are cleaned by Hoovers than by any other cleaner. . . . *Hoover is the oldest* maker of electric cleaners and the largest. More than 3,000,000 Hoovers have been sold. . . . *The Hoover is unique* due to its exclusive, patented cleaning principle, Positive Agitation. By gently beating the rug, The Hoover dislodges even the most deeply embedded grit so injurious to rugs, and removes it along with lint, hair, litter and dust. . . . It is recommended by leading rug manufacturers for the cleaning and care of floor coverings. . . . *The Hoover* is not only more efficient at the start, but is kept efficient by its sturdier construction. . . . *The Hoover, complete with Dusting Tools or Dustette,* may be bought on as low a down payment and with as small an outlay per month as the cheapest machine, yet a Hoover brings you many more years of cleaning service. . . . *The Hoover is sold* and endorsed by the leading merchants of the country. Open your door with confidence to their bonded and trustworthy representatives. . . . The Hoover man will be glad to leave any of the three new Hoovers for a no-obligation home trial. *The Hoover Co. Factories: North Canton, Ohio; Hamilton, Ontario.*

The **HOOVER**
It Beats . . . as it Sweeps . . . as it Cleans

A democratic consumer revolution: Hoover advertisement, February 1933

Sears, Roebuck catalogue, spring 1934

War, Westerners, and in particular Americans, became the most privileged, and most harried, consumers on the planet.

Across the United States, new longings were created by the development of shopping malls, which enabled citizens to browse at all hours in climate-controlled environments. When the Southdale Mall opened in Minnesota in 1950, its advertising promised that "every day will be a perfect shopping day at Southdale."

By the 1970s, Americans were estimated to be spending more time at the mall than anywhere else other than their workplaces and their Taj Mahals.

Andreas Gursky, 99 cents, *2000*

Equality, Expectation and Envy

1.

The benefits of two thousand years of Western civilization are familiar enough: an extraordinary increase in wealth, in food supply, in scientific knowledge, in the availability of consumer goods, in physical security, in life expectancy and economic opportunity. What is perhaps less apparent, and more perplexing, is that these impressive material advances have coincided with a phenomenon left unmentioned in Nixon's address to his Soviet audience: a rise in the levels of status anxiety among ordinary Western citizens, by which is meant a rise in levels of concern about importance, achievement and income.

A sharp decline in *actual* deprivation may, paradoxically, have been accompanied by an ongoing and even escalating *sense* or *fear* of deprivation. Blessed with riches and possibilities far beyond anything imagined by ancestors who tilled the unpredictable soil of medieval Europe, modern populations have nonetheless shown a remarkable capacity to feel that neither who they are nor what they have is quite enough.

2.

Such feelings of deprivation may seem less peculiar if we consider the psychology behind the way we decide precisely *how much* is enough. Our judgement of what constitutes an appropriate limit on anything—for example, on wealth or esteem—is never arrived at independently; instead, we make such determinations by comparing our condition with that of a reference group, a set of people who we believe resemble us. We cannot, it seems, appreciate what we have for its own merit, or even against what our medieval forebears had. We cannot be impressed by how prosperous we are in historical terms. We see ourselves as fortunate only when we have as much as, or more than, those we have grown up with, work alongside, have as friends or identify with in the public realm.

If we are made to live in a draughty, insalubrious cottage and bend to the harsh rule of an aristocrat occupying a large and well-heated castle, and yet we observe that our equals all live exactly as we do, then our condition will seem normal—regrettable, certainly, but not a fertile ground for envy. If, however, we have a pleasant home and a comfortable job but learn through ill-advised attendance at a school reunion that some of our old friends (there is no more compelling reference group) now reside in houses grander than ours, bought on the salaries they are paid in more enticing occupations than our own, we are likely to return home nursing a violent sense of misfortune.

It is the feeling that we might, under different circumstances, be something other than what we are—a feeling inspired by exposure to the superior achievements of those whom we take to be our equals—that generates anxiety and resentment. If we are short, say, but live among people of our same height, we will not be unduly troubled by questions of size:

But if others in our group grow just a little taller than us, we are liable to feel sudden unease and to be gripped by dissatisfaction and envy, even though we have not ourselves diminished in size by so much as a fraction of a millimetre.

Given the vast inequalities we are daily confronted with, the most notable feature of envy may be that we manage not to envy *everyone*. There are people whose enormous blessings leave us wholly untroubled, even as others' negligible advantages become a source of relentless torment for us. We envy only those whom we feel ourselves to be like—we envy only members of our reference group. There are few successes more unendurable than those of our ostensible equals.

3.

David Hume, *A Treatise on Human Nature* (Edinburgh, 1739): "It is not a great disproportion between ourselves and others which produces envy, but on the contrary, a proximity. A common soldier bears no envy for his general compared to what he will feel for his sergeant or corporal; nor does an eminent writer meet with as much jealousy in common hackney scribblers, as in authors that more nearly approach him. A great disproportion cuts off the relation, and either keeps us from comparing ourselves with what is remote from us or diminishes the effects of the comparison."

4.

It follows that the greater the number of people whom we take to be our equals and compare ourselves to, the more there will be for us to envy.

If the great political and consumer revolutions of the eighteenth and nineteenth centuries caused psychological anguish while vastly improving the material lot of mankind, it was because they were founded on a set of extraordinary new ideals, a practical belief in the innate equality of all human beings and in the unlimited power of any*one* to achieve any*thing*. For most of history, the opposite assumption had held sway, with inequality and low expectations being deemed both normal and wise. Very few among the masses had ever aspired to wealth or fulfilment; the rest knew well enough that they were condemned to exploitation and resignation.

"It is clear that some men are by nature free and others are by nature slaves, and that for these latter, slavery is both expedient and right," Aristotle declared in his *Politics* (350 B.C.), voicing an opinion shared by almost all Greek and Roman thinkers and leaders. In the ancient world, slaves and the members of the working classes in general were considered to be not truly human at all but a species of creature, lacking in reason and therefore perfectly fitted to a life of servitude, just as beasts of burden were suited to tilling fields. The notion that they might have rights and aspirations of their own would have been judged by the elite no less absurd than, say, an expression of concern for the thought processes or level of happiness of an ox or an ass.

The belief that inequality was fair, or at least inescapable, was also subscribed to by the oppressed themselves. With the spread of Christianity during the later Roman Empire, many fell prey to a religion that taught them to accept unequal treatment as part of a natural, unchangeable order. Notwithstanding the egalitarian principles embedded within Christ's teachings, there was little suggestion on the part of Christian political theorists that the earthly social structure could or should be reformed so that all members of the Church might share more equitably in the wealth of the land. Humans might be equal before God, but this offered no reason to start seeking equality in practice.

For these theorists, a good Christian society instead took the form of a rigidly stratified monarchy, a design said to reflect the ordering of the celestial kingdom. Just as God wielded absolute power over all creation, from the angels down to the smallest toads, so, too, his appointed rulers on earth were understood to preside over a society where God had given everyone his and her place, from the nobleman down to the farm-hand. To have accused a medieval

A medieval vision of hierarchy: Jacobello del Fiore,
The Coronation of the Virgin in Paradise, *1438*

English aristocrat of "snobbery" for his attitudes to those below him in the hierarchy would have made no sense. A derogatory term for segregation could make an appearance only once a more egalitarian way of looking at people had come to seem a possibility.

Sir John Fortescue, a fifteenth-century English jurist, was merely restating an idea taken for granted throughout the medieval period when he explained, "From the highest angel down to the lowest, there is no angel that is without both a superior and inferior; nor from man down to the meanest worm is there any creature which is not in some respect superior to one creature and inferior to another." To challenge why some were compelled to till the soil while others feasted in banqueting halls was, in the dominant ideology, to challenge the Creator's will.

With his *Policraticus* (1159), John of Salisbury had become the most famous Christian writer to compare society to a human body and to use that analogy to justify a system of natural inequality. In Salisbury's formulation, every element in the state had an anatomical counterpart: the ruler was the head, the parliament was the heart, the court was the sides, officials and judges were the eyes, ears and tongue, the treasury was the belly and intestines, the army was the hands and the peasantry and labouring classes were the feet. This image reinforced the concept that every member of society had been assigned an unalterable role, a scheme that made it no less ludicrous for a peasant to wish to take up residence in a manor house and have a say in his own governance than for a toe to aspire to be an eye.

5.

Only in the middle of the seventeenth century did political thinking begin to venture in a more egalitarian direction.

In *Leviathan* (1651), Thomas Hobbes contended that the individual predated society and had formed and joined it for his own benefit, willingly surrendering his natural rights in exchange for the protection offered by a group or sovereign. This seminal point would be reiterated a few decades later by John Locke in his *Two Treatises of Government* (1689). God had not, Locke reasoned, bestowed on Adam "private dominion" over the earth; rather, he had given the world "to mankind in common," for the enjoyment of all. Rulers were the instruments of the people and were fit to be obeyed only insofar as they served their subjects' interest. Thus was born an astonishing new idea: that governments justify their existence only by promoting possibilities for prosperity and happiness among all those they rule over.

The theoretical impulse towards political equality and more equitable social and economic opportunities for all, after being in the ether for a century and a half, finally found dramatic, concrete expression in the American Revolution of 1776. Perhaps more than any other event in Western history (even the French Revolution that would succeed it), the "War for Independence" altered forever the basis upon which status was accorded. In a stroke, it transformed American society from a hereditary, aristocratic hierarchy—a sphere in which upward mobility was restricted and a person's status depended exclusively on the lineage and distinction of his or her family—into a dynamic economy in which status was awarded in direct proportion to the (largely financial) achievements of each new generation.

By 1791, the geographer Jedidiah Morse could describe New England as a place "where every man thinks himself at least as good as his neighbours, and believes that all mankind have, or ought to possess, equal rights." Even etiquette was democratised. Servants (though not slaves) had ceased addressing their employers as "master" or "mistress," and in Charleston, South Carolina, the city council had banned the use of the titles "Esq." and "His Honour." All American states legislated against primogeniture and granted equal property rights to daughters and widows. The physician-historian David Ramsay, in his "Oration on the Advantages of American Independence," delivered on 4 July 1778, proposed that the goal of the Revolution had been to establish a society in which "all offices lie open to men of merit of whatever rank or condition. Even the reins of state may be held by the son of the poorest man, if he is possessed of abilities that are equal to this important station." In his autobiography, Thomas Jefferson avowed that his own energies had been directed towards creating "an opening for the aristocracy of virtue and talent" to replace the old culture of privilege and, in many cases, brute stupidity.

Decades later, in *Leaves of Grass* (1855), Walt Whitman would identify the greatness of America specifically with equality and its citizenry's native lack of deference: "The genius of the United States is not best or most in its executives or legislatures, nor in its ambassadors or authors or colleges or churches or parlours, nor even in its newspapers or inventors . . . but always most in the common people . . . the air they have of persons who never knew how it felt to stand in the presence of superiors . . . the terrible significance of their elections—the President's taking off his hat to them not they to him . . ."

6.

Still, even enthusiastic admirers of consumer and democratic revolutions could not help but notice a particular problem that seemed to be endemic to the equal societies they created. One of the first to point it out was Alexis de Tocqueville.

Touring the young United States in the 1830s, the French lawyer and historian discerned an unexpected ill corroding the souls of the citizens of the new republic. Americans had much, he observed, but their affluence did not prevent them from wanting ever more or from suffering whenever they saw that another had something they themselves didn't. In a chapter of *Democracy in America* (1835) entitled "Why the Americans Are Often So Restless in the Midst of Their Prosperity," he provided an enduring analysis of the relationships between dissatisfaction and high expectation, between envy and equality:

"When all prerogatives of birth and fortune have been abolished, when every profession is open to everyone . . . an ambitious man may think it is easy to launch himself on a great career and feel that he has been called to no common destiny. But this is a delusion which experience quickly corrects. When inequality is the general rule in society, the greatest inequalities attract no attention. But when everything is more or less level, the slightest variation is noticed . . . That is the reason for the strange melancholy often haunting inhabitants of democracies in the midst of abundance and of that disgust with life sometimes gripping them even in calm and easy circumstances. In France, we are worried about increasing rate of suicides. In America, suicide is rare, but I am told that madness is commoner than anywhere else."

Familiar with the limitations of aristocratic societies, Tocqueville felt no nostalgia for the social conditions that had prevailed in America prior to 1776 or in France before 1789. He knew that the populations of the modern West boasted a standard of living far higher than that of the lower classes of medieval Europe. Nevertheless, he suspected that these deprived classes had also had the benefit of a mental calm that their successors would be forever denied:

"When royal power supported by aristocracies governed nations, society, despite all its wretchedness, enjoyed several types of happiness which are difficult to appreciate today. Having never conceived the possibility of a social state other than the one they knew, and never expecting to become equal to their leaders, the people did not question their rights. They felt neither repugnance nor degradation in submitting to severities, which seemed to them like inevitable ills sent by God. The serf considered his inferiority as an effect of the immutable order of nature. Consequently, a sort of goodwill was established between classes so differently favoured by fortune. One found inequality in society, but men's souls were not degraded thereby."

Democracy, by definition, tore down every barrier to expectation. All members of a democratic society perceived themselves as being theoretically equal, even where the means was lacking to achieve material equality. "In America," wrote Tocqueville, "I never met a citizen too poor to cast a glance of hope and envy toward the pleasures of the rich." The poor citizens observed rich ones at close quarters and trusted that they too would one day follow in their footsteps. They were not always wrong. A number of fortunes were made by people from humble beginnings. Exceptions did not, however, make a rule. America still had an underclass. It was just that, unlike the poor of aristocratic societies, poor Americans could no longer see their condition as anything other than a betrayal of their expectations.

The differing notions of poverty within aristocratic and democratic societies were especially evident, Tocqueville felt, in the attitude of servants towards their masters. In aristocracies, servants often accepted their position with good grace; it was not impossible for them to harbour, in Tocqueville's words, "high thoughts, strong pride and self-respect." In democracies, by contrast, the propaganda of the press and public opinion relentlessly promised servants that they, too, could reach the pinnacles of society and make their fortune as industrialists, judges, scientists or even presidents. Although this sense of unbounded opportunity could initially excite a surface cheerfulness in them—particularly in the younger ones—and though it did encourage the most talented or luckiest among them to fulfil their goals, as time passed and the majority failed to raise themselves, Tocqueville noted that their mood darkened, bitterness took hold of and choked their spirit, and their hatred of themselves and their masters grew fierce.

The rigid hierarchy that had been in place in almost every Western society until the late eighteenth century, denying all hope of social movement except in the rarest of cases, the system glorified by John of Salisbury and John Fortescue, was unjust in a thousand all too obvious ways, but it offered those on the lowest rungs one notable freedom: the freedom not to have to take the achievements of quite so many people in society as reference points—and so find themselves severely wanting in status and importance as a result.

7.

It was an American, William James, who, a few decades after Tocqueville's journey around the United States, first looked from a psychological angle at the problems created by societies which generate unlimited expectations in their members.

James argued that one's ability to feel satisfied with oneself does not hang on experiencing success in every area of endeavour. We are not always humiliated by failing at things, he suggested; we are humiliated only if we invest our pride and sense of worth in a given aspiration or achievement and then are disappointed in our pursuit of it. Our goals dictate what we will interpret as a triumph and what must count as a catastrophe. James himself, for example, as a professor of psychology at Harvard, took a great deal of pride in being a prominent psychologist. If he should discover that others knew more about psychology than he did, he would, he admitted, feel envy and shame. Conversely, because he had never set himself the task of learning ancient Greek, the knowledge that someone else could translate the whole of Plato's *Symposium* whereas he struggled with the opening line was of little concern to him. He explained:

"With no attempt there can be no failure; with no failure no humiliation. So our self-esteem in this world depends entirely on what we *back* ourselves to be and do. It is determined by the ratio of our actualities to our supposed potentialities. Thus:

$$\text{Self-esteem} = \frac{\text{Success}}{\text{Pretensions}}"$$

James's equation illustrates how every rise in our levels of expectation entails a rise in the dangers of humiliation. What we understand to be normal is critical in determining our chances of happiness. Few things rival the torment of the once-famous actor, the fallen politician or, as Tocqueville might have remarked, the unsuccessful American.

The equation also hints at two manoeuvres for raising our self-esteem. On the one hand, we may try to achieve more; and on the other, we may reduce the number of things we want to achieve. James pointed to the advantages of the latter approach:

"To give up pretensions is as blessed a relief as to get them gratified. There is a strange lightness in the heart when one's nothingness in a particular area is accepted in good faith. How pleasant is the day when we give up striving to be young or slender. 'Thank God!' we say, '*those* illusions are gone.' Everything added to the self is a burden as well as a pride."

8.

Unfortunately for our esteem, societies of the West are not known for their conduciveness to the surrender of pretensions, to the acceptance of age or fat, let alone poverty and obscurity. Their mood urges us to invest ourselves in activities and belongings that our predecessors would have had no thought of. According to James's equation, by greatly increasing our pretensions, these societies render adequate self-esteem almost impossible to secure.

The dangers of disappointed expectation must further be increased by any erosion of a faith in a next world. Those who can believe that what happens on earth is but a brief prelude to an eternal existence will offset any tendency to envy with the thought that the success of others is a momentary phenomenon against a backdrop of an eternal life.

But when a belief in an afterlife is dismissed as a childish and scientifically impossible opiate, the pressure to succeed and find fulfilment will inevitably be intensified by the awareness that one has only a single and frighteningly fleeting opportunity to do so. In such a context, earthly achievements can no longer be seen as an overture to what one may realize in another world; rather, they are the sum total of all that one will ever amount to.

Resignation regarding the necessary hardships of life was for centuries one of mankind's most important assets, a bulwark against bitterness that was to be cruelly undermined by the expectations incubated by the modern worldview. In his *City of God* (A.D. 427), Saint Augustine consolingly codified unhappiness as an immutable feature of existence, part of "the wretchedness of man's situation," and poured scorn on "all those theories by which men have tried hard to build up joy for themselves within the misery of this life." Under Augustine's influence, the French poet Eustache Deschamps (circa 1338–1410) described life on earth as a

Time of mourning and of temptation,
An age of tears, of envy and of torment,
A time of languor and of damnation . . .

Temps de doleur et de temptacion,
Aages de plour, d'envie et de tourment,
Temps de langour et de dampnacion . . .

When informed of the death of his one-year-old son, Philippe the Good (1396–1467), duke of Burgundy, replied in a tone characteristic of many voices in the premodern period: "If only God had deigned to let me die so young, I would have considered myself fortunate."

9.

But the modern age has been less liberal—and less kind—with its pessimism.

Since the early nineteenth century, Western writers and publishers have endeavoured to inspire—and in the process have unintentionally saddened—their readers with autobiographies of self-made heroes and compendia of advice directed at the not-yet-made, morality tales of wholesale personal transformation and the rapid attainment of vast wealth and great happiness.

Benjamin Franklin's *Autobiography* (left incomplete at his death, in 1790) was perhaps the progenitor of the genre, recounting how a penniless young man, one of seventeen children of a Boston candle maker, had ended up accruing, entirely by his wits, not only a fortune but the friendship and respect of some of the most important people of his day. Franklin's history of self-improvement, and the analects he drew from it ("Early to Bed, and early to rise, makes a Man healthy, wealthy and wise"; "There are no gains without pains"), belonged to a vast literature intended to edify readers possessed of modest means and grand ambitions. Among the countless later titles in this category were William Mathews's *Getting On in the*

World (1874), William Maher's *On the Road to Riches* (1876), Edwin T. Freedley's *The Secret of Success in Life* (1881), Lyman Abbott's *How to Succeed* (1882), William Speer's *The Law of Success* (1885) and Samuel Fallows's *The Problem of Success for Young Men and How to Solve It* (1903).

The trend has not abated. "Right now you can make a decision," explained Anthony Robbins (*Awaken the Giant Within,* 1991), "to go back to school, to master dancing or singing, to take control of your finances, to learn to fly a helicopter. . . . If you truly decide to, you can do almost anything. So if you don't like the current relationship you're in, make the decision now to change it. If you don't like your current job, change it."

Robbins offered his own story as evidence that radical transformation was possible. He had risen from humble and unhappy origins: in his early twenties, he worked as a janitor and lived in a small, dirty apartment. Forty pounds overweight, he had no girlfriend and spent his evenings alone at home listening to Neil Diamond. Then, one day, he abruptly resolved to revolutionise his life and discovered a mental "power" that would enable him to do so:

"I used [this power] to take back control of my physical well-being and permanently rid myself of thirty-eight pounds of fat. Through it, I attracted the woman of my dreams, married her and created the family I desired. I used this power to change my income from subsistence level to over one million dollars a year. It moved me from my tiny apartment (where I was washing my dishes in the bathtub because there was no kitchen) to my family's current home, the Del Mar Castle."

Anyone, Robbins assured his audience, could follow his example, but most particularly those lucky enough to live in democratic and capitalist societies, in which "we all have the capability to carry out our dreams."

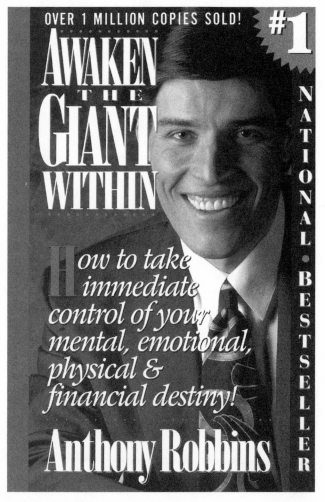

Anthony Robbins, Awaken the Giant Within, *1991*

10.

The burgeoning of the mass media from the late nineteenth century helped to raise expectations even higher. At his newspaper's launch in 1896, Alfred Harmsworth, the founder of Britain's *Daily Mail*, candidly characterised his ideal reader as a man in the street "worth one hundred pounds per annum" who could be enticed to dream of being "tomorrow's thousand pound man." In America, meanwhile, the *Ladies' Home Journal* (first published in 1883), *Cosmopolitan* (1886), *Munsey's* (1889) and *Vogue* (1892) brought an expensive life within the imaginative reach of all. Readers of fin de siècle American *Vogue*, for example, were told who had been aboard *Nourmahal*, John Jacob Astor's yacht, after the America's Cup race, what the most fashionable young ladies were wearing at boarding school, who threw the best parties in Newport and Southampton and what to serve with caviar at dinner (potato and sour cream).

The opportunity to study the lives of people of higher status and forge a connection with them was also increased by the development of radio, film and television. By the 1930s, Americans were collectively spending some 150 million hours per week at the cinema and almost a billion hours listening to the radio. In 1946, 0.02 percent of American households owned television sets; by 2000, the figure stood at 98 percent.

The new media created longings not only through their content but also through the advertisements they imposed on their audiences. From its amateurish beginnings in the United States in the 1830s, advertising had by the end of the nineteenth century grown into a business worth $500 million a year. In 1900, a giant Coca-Cola sign was erected on one side of Niagara Falls, while an advert for Mennen's Toilet Powder was suspended over the gorge.

11.

When defenders of modern societies have sought to make a case to sceptics, their task has not been difficult: they have had only to point to the enormous wealth that modern societies are able to generate for their members.

In his *Inquiry into the Nature and Causes of the Wealth of Nations* (1776), Adam Smith sarcastically compared the awe-inspiring productivity of proto-industrial societies with the bare subsistence of primitive hunting-and-gathering ones. The latter were, by Smith's account, steeped in terrible poverty. Harvests rarely yielded enough food, there were chronic shortages of basic necessities and, in times of serious crisis, children, the elderly and the poor were often left "to be devoured by wild beasts." Modern societies, in contrast, thanks to their innovative mode of production—described by Smith as "the division of labour"—could provide for *all* their members. Only a romantic ignoramus could wish to live anywhere else; in such a society "a workman, even of the lowest and poorest order, if he is frugal and industrious, may enjoy a greater share of the necessaries and conveniences of life than it is possible for any savage to acquire."

12.

However, twenty-two years before the publication of Smith's treatise, a lone, shrill, eccentric yet unsettlingly persuasive voice had been raised in defense of an unlikely hero: the savage. Was it possible, asked Jean-Jacques Rousseau in his *Discourse on the Origin of Inequality* (1754), that it was in fact the hunter-gatherer and not, as everyone had grown used to believing, the modern worker who was the better off?

Rousseau's argument hung on a radical thesis. Being truly wealthy, he suggested, does not require having many things; rather, it requires having what one *longs* for. Wealth is not an absolute. It is relative to desire. Every time we yearn for something we cannot afford, we grow poorer, whatever our resources. And every time we feel satisfied with what we have, we can be counted as rich, however little we may actually possess.

There are two ways to make a man richer, reasoned Rousseau: give him more money or curb his desires. Modern societies have done the former spectacularly well, but by continuously whetting appetites, they have at the same time managed to negate a share of their success. For the individual, trying to make more money may not be the most effective way to feel wealthy. We might do better, instead, to distance ourselves, both practically and emotionally, from those whom we consider to be our equals and yet who have grown richer than us. Rather than struggling to become bigger fish, we might concentrate our energies on finding smaller ponds or smaller species to swim with, so our own size will trouble us less.

Insofar as advanced societies supply their members with historically elevated incomes, they appear to make us wealthier. But in truth, their net effect may be to impoverish us, because by fostering unlimited expectations, they keep open permanent gaps between what we want and what we can afford, between who we might be and who we really are. Such disparities may leave us feeling more deprived even than primitive savages, who, insisted Rousseau (his argument here reaching the limits of plausibility), felt themselves to be lacking for nothing in the world so long as they had a roof over their heads, a few apples and nuts to eat and the leisure to spend their evenings playing on "some crude musical instrument" or "using sharp-edged stones to make a fishing canoe."

Rousseau's comparison of the relative levels of happiness of primitive and modern man returns us to William James's emphasis on the role of expectations in determining our quotient of self-esteem. We may be happy enough with little if little is what we have come to expect, and we may be miserable with much when we have been taught to desire everything.

Rousseau's naked savages had few possessions. But, unlike their successors in their Taj Mahals, they were at least able to feast on the great wealth that comes from aspiring to very little.

13.

The price we have paid for expecting to be so much more than our ancestors is a perpetual anxiety that we are far from being all we might be.

III
MERITOCRACY

Three Useful Old Stories about Failure

1.

To occupy a low position in the social hierarchy is rarely pleasant from a material point of view, but it is not everywhere and at all times equally psychologically painful. The impact of poverty on self-esteem will to an important extent be decided by the way that poverty is interpreted and accounted for by the community.

While the material progress of the West over two millennia is incontestable, explanations for why one might be poor and what one's value to society might be, could be said to have grown notably more punitive and emotionally awkward in the modern era, an evolution contributing a third explanation for any anxiety about having or acquiring low status.

2.

From approximately A.D. 30, when Jesus began his ministry, to the latter half of the twentieth century, the lowest in Western societies had to hand three stories about their significance, which, while they could be believed, must have worked a profoundly consoling, anxiety-reducing effect on their listeners.

First Story:
The Poor Are Not Responsible for Their Condition and Are the Most Useful in Society

If one had asked a member of a Western medieval or pre-modern society on what basis society was divided into rich and poor, peasant

A representation of the three orders of society—clergy, nobility and peasantry—from the Image du Monde. *French school, thirteenth century*

and nobleman, the question would most likely have seemed bizarre: God had simply willed the division.

Yet alongside this inflexible belief in a three-class structure—clergy, nobility and peasantry—came an unusually strong appreciation of the way that the different classes depended on each other and hence an unusually strong appreciation of the value of the poorest class. A theory of mutual dependence held that the peasantry was no less vital and hence no less worthy of dignity than the nobility or clergy. The lives of peasants might be hard (unalterably so), but it was known that without them the other two classes would soon founder. It might have seemed ungenerous of John of Salisbury to compare the poor to a pair of feet and the rich to a head, but this otherwise insulting metaphor had the benefit of reminding the wealthy to treat the poor with respect if they wanted to stay alive just as they knew to treat their feet with respect in order to walk.

Patronisation was accompanied by its more advantageous twin, paternalism: if the poor were like children, then it was the task of the rich to assume the role of loving parents. Medieval art and literature were therefore peppered with liberal, if condescending, praise of the peasantry, and it was not forgotten that Jesus himself had been a carpenter.

In his *Colloquy* (circa 1015), Aelfric, the abbot of Eynsham, argued that peasants were the most important members of society by far, for though the rest could survive without the nobility or the clergy, no one could do without the food supplied by the ploughman. In 1036, Bishop Gerard of Cambrai preached a sermon asserting that while such rough labour was dull and hard, it made possible all other, intellectually more elevated, kinds of work. Good people must thus honour the peasantry. Hans Rosenplüt of Nuremberg was one poet among many who felt moved to pay homage to the "noble ploughman." In his poem "Der Bauern Lob" (circa 1450), he intoned that in all God's creation, none was more exalted:

It is often hard labour for him when he
   wields the plough
With which he feeds all the world:
   lords, townsmen and artisans.
But if there were no peasant, our
   lives would be in a very sad
   condition.

A peasant reaping wheat, from a psalter
calendar, England, circa 1250–1275

49

Such words may not have softened the earth through which the peasants had to drive their plough, but when considered together with the attitude underlying them, they must nevertheless have helped to foster in the peasantry a welcome sense of their own dignity.

The Limbourg Brothers, Peasants at Work on a Feudal Estate, *1400–1416*

Second Story:
Low Status Has No Moral Connotation

Scripture provided another comforting perspective for those of low status. The New Testament demonstrated that neither wealth nor poverty was an accurate index of moral worth. After all, Jesus was the highest man, the most blessed, and yet on earth he had been poor, ruling out any simple equation between righteousness and riches.

Insofar as Christianity ever strayed from a neutral position on money, it was in favour of poverty, for in the Christian schema, the source of all goodness was the recognition of one's dependence on God. Anything that encouraged the belief that a contented life might be had without God's grace was evil, and wealth fell into that category, promising both worldly pleasures and a frowned-upon sense of freedom.

The hardships to which the poor were subject, meanwhile, made them turn more naturally to God for assistance. In the soothing parables of the New Testament, they witnessed the rich failing to fit through the eyes of needles, learned that they would inherit the earth and were assured that they would be among the first through the gates of the Heavenly Kingdom.

Third Story:
The Rich Are Sinful and Corrupt
and Owe Their Wealth to Their Robbery of the Poor

There was a third story available to soften the blow of poverty and a low social position. According to this narrative, which assumed its greatest influence between approximately 1754 and 1989, the poor were reminded that the rich were thieving and corrupt and had attained their privileges through plunder and deception rather than virtue or talent. Moreover, they had rigged society in such a way that the poor could never improve their lot individually, however capable and willing they might be. Their only hope lay in mass social protest and revolution.

In his *Discourse on the Origin of Inequality* (1754), Jean-Jacques Rousseau gave the story one of its earliest recitals: "The first person who, having enclosed a plot of land, took it into his head to say *this is mine* and found people simple enough to believe him, was the true founder of civil society. What crimes, wars, murders, what miseries and horrors would the human race have been spared, had someone pulled up the stakes or filled in the ditch and cried out to his fellow men: 'Do not listen to this impostor. You are lost if you forget that the fruits of the earth belong to all and the earth to no one!'"

A hundred years later, Karl Marx would take up the same cry, casting in apparently scientific terms what had in Rousseau's hands been a cry of social protest. There was, for Marx, an inherently exploitative dynamic within the capitalist system, for employers would always try to hire workers for less than they made from selling their products, then would pocket the difference as "profit." Such profit was invariably hailed in the capitalist press as the employers' reward for "risk-taking" and "enterprise," but Marx insisted that these words were mere euphemisms for theft.

The bourgeoisie, by this account, was merely the latest incarnation of a master class that had unjustly held sway over the poor since the beginning of time. However humane its members might seem, a civilized surface concealed a calculating ruthlessness. In the first volume of *Capital* (1887), Marx addressed the bourgeoisie in the voice of the worker: "You may be a model citizen, perhaps a member of the Society for the Prevention of Cruelty to Animals, and have the odour of sanctity to boot, but you are a creature with no heart in its breast." Evidence of this callousness could be found in any nineteenth-century mill, bakery, dockyard, hotel or office. Workers were diseased and very often died young of cancer or respiratory illness; their jobs denied them any hope of a proper family life, left them no time to develop an intellectual understanding of their position and left them anxious and without security: "for all its stinginess, capitalist production is thoroughly wasteful with human material." So Marx urged the "human material" to rise up against its masters and reclaim what it was rightfully owed. As *The Communist Manifesto* (1848) thundered, "Let the ruling classes tremble at a communist revolution. The proletarians have nothing to lose but their chains. They have a world to win. WORKINGMEN OF ALL COUNTRIES, UNITE!"

Not long before the publication of the *Manifesto*, Marx's associate Friedrich Engels had travelled to Manchester and seen at first hand the suffering of the poor in one of the new cities of the Industrial Revolution. Engels shared his colleague's conviction as to why society was split into classes: the rich were rich, he believed, not because they were clever or energetic or diligent but because they were cunning and mean. And the poor were poor not because they were idle or drunk or dim but because they had been blindfolded and abused by their masters. The bourgeoisie depicted in Engels's account of his sojourn, *The Condition of the Working-Class in England* (1845), took self-interest to sobering extremes: "It is money gain which alone determines them. I once went into Manchester with a bourgeois, and spoke to him of the bad, unwholesome method of building, the frightful condition of the working-people's quarters, and asserted that I had never seen so ill-built a city. The man listened quietly to the end, and then said at the corner where we parted: 'And yet there is a great deal of money made here. Good morning, sir.' It is utterly indifferent to the English bourgeois whether his working-men starve or not, if only he makes money. All the conditions of life are measured by money, and what brings no money is nonsense, unpractical, idealistic bosh."

Life may not have been pleasant in the slums of Manchester in the 1840s, but for a labourer, being advised that what had landed him there was the monstrosity of his employer and the endemic corruption of the economic system (against which it was vain for the poor ever to try to act singly) would have offered a sustaining sense of his moral superiority and mitigated any shame he might have felt at his haggard condition.

3.

In their different ways, these three stories afforded consolation for low status over nearly two millennia. They were by no means the only stories in circulation, but they had power and were widely credited. They oriented the less fortunate towards three sustaining ideas: that they were the true creators of wealth in society and therefore were deserving of respect; that earthly status had no moral value in the eyes of God; and that the rich were in any case not worth honouring, for they were both unscrupulous and destined to meet a bad end in a series of imminent and just proletarian revolutions.

Three Anxiety-Inducing New Stories about Success

1.

Unfortunately, three other, more troubling stories began to form around the middle of the eighteenth century and steadily gained in influence, challenging the previous stories in public opinion.

The rise of these stories may have been accompanied by momentous material improvements across society, but at a psychological level, their contribution was to make low status all the harder to endure and all the more worrying to contemplate.

First Story:
The Rich Are the Useful Ones, Not the Poor

Writing in circa 1015, Aelfric, the abbot of Eynsham, had emphasized that wealth was created almost exclusively by the poor, who rose before dawn, ploughed the fields and collected the harvests. The critical nature of their work gave them a right to be honoured by all those above them in the hierarchy. The abbot was not alone in thus recognising ordinary workers: for centuries, economic orthodoxy held that it was the working classes that generated society's financial resources—which the rich then dissipated through their taste for extravagance and luxury.

This of who could be credited for creating national wealth theory survived almost unassailed until the spring of 1723, when a London physician named Bernard Mandeville published an economic tract in verse, *The Fable of the Bees,* which irrevocably altered the way rich and poor were perceived. Mandeville posited that, contrary to centuries of economic thinking, it was the *rich* who in fact contributed the most to society, insofar as their spending provided employment for everyone below them and so helped the weakest to survive. Without the rich, the poor would soon be laid out in their graves. Mandeville did not wish to suggest that the rich were *nicer* than the poor—in fact, he gleefully pointed out how vain, cruel and fickle they could be. Their desires knew no bounds, they craved applause and failed to understand that happiness did not have its origins in material acquisition. And yet their pursuit and attainment of wealth were of infinitely greater use to society than the patient, unremunerative work of labourers. In judging a man's value, one had to look not at his soul (as Christian moralists were inclined to do) but at his impact on others. Judged by this new criterion, those who amassed riches (in trade, industry or agriculture) and spent liberally (on absurd luxuries or on the construction of unnecessary storehouses or country seats) were without question more beneficially engaged than the poor. As the subtitle of Mandeville's opus put it, it was a case of "Private Vices, Public Benefits." He explained: "It is the sensual courtier who sets no limit to his luxury, the fickle strumpet who invents new fashions every week . . . the profuse rake and the lavish heir [who most effectively help the poor]. He that gives most trouble to thousands of his neighbours, and invents the most operose manufactures is, right or wrong, the greatest friend to society. Mercers, upholsterers, tailors and many others would be starved in half a year's time if *pride* and *luxury* were at once to be banished from the nation."

Although Mandeville's thesis shocked his initial audience (as he intended it to do), it would go on to persuade almost all the great economists and political thinkers of the eighteenth century and beyond. In his essay "Of Luxury" (1752), Hume repeated the Mandevilleian argument in favour of the pursuit of riches and their expenditure on superfluous goods, asserting that it was these initiatives, rather than the manual labour of the poor, that produced wealth: "In a nation . . . where there is no demand for superfluities, men sink into indolence, lose all enjoyment of life, and are useless to the public, which cannot maintain or support its fleets and armies."

Seven years later, Hume's countryman Adam Smith would take the proposition even further in his *Theory of Moral Sentiments,* perhaps the most beguiling defence ever assayed of the utility of the rich. Smith began by admitting that great sums of money did not always bring happiness: "Riches leave a man always as much and sometimes more exposed than before to anxiety, to fear and to sorrow." He went on caustically to dismiss those foolish enough to devote their entire lives to chasing "baubles and trinkets." Nevertheless, he was, he noted, immensely grateful that such creatures abounded, for the whole of civilisation, and the welfare of all societies, depended on people's desire and ability to accumulate unneeded capital and show off their wealth. Indeed, it was this "which first prompted men to cultivate the ground, to build houses, to found cities and commonwealths and to invent all the sciences and arts which ennoble and embellish human life; which have entirely changed the whole face of the globe, have turned the rude forests of nature into agreeable and fertile plains, and made the trackless and barren ocean a new fund of subsistence."

In economic theories of old, the rich had been condemned for consuming too large a share of what was thought to be a finite pool of national wealth. But tempting though it might seem, Smith wrote, to regard man of "huge estate" as a "pest to society, as a monster, a great fish who devours up all the lesser ones," to do this was to forget that there was no predetermined limit to the pool of wealth, which could always be expanded through the efforts and ambitions of entrepreneurs and traders. The great fish and his brethren, far from devouring the lesser fish, in practice helped them by spending money and ensuring them of employment. The rich might be arrogant and coarse, but their vices were transformed, through the operations of the marketplace, into virtues—or so Smith claimed in what has become possibly the most famous passage in the literature of capitalist economics: "In spite of their natural selfishness and rapacity, though they mean only their own convenience, though the sole end which they propose from the labours of all the thousands whom they employ be the gratification of their own vain and insatiable desires, the rich divide with the poor the produce of all their improvements. They are led by an invisible hand to make nearly the same distribution of the necessities of life, which would have been made, had the earth been divided into equal portions among all its inhabitants, and thus, without intending it, without knowing it, advance the interest of the society, and afford means to the multiplication of the species."

Indeed, in societies in which the wealthy were given sufficient opportunities to trade and develop industry, "so great a quantity of everything is produced," wrote Smith, "that there is enough both to gratify the slothful and oppressive profusions of the great and at the same time abundantly to supply the wants of the artisan and peasant."

Here, then, was an unexpectedly delightful story for the better off. The villains of economic theory since the early days of Christianity, they now found themselves recast as its heroes. It was the wealthiest who deserved praise for helping all the other social classes; it was the rich who housed the poor and fed the needy; it was the great fish that provided for the little fish swimming in their wake. Furthermore, they did all this even when they were personally reprehensible—in fact, the greedier they were, the better.

The story was less flattering to the poor. While the rich were hailed as creators of national prosperity, the poor were credited with only a modest, functional contribution; on occasion, they were even accused of *draining* resources through their excessive numbers and reliance on welfare and charity. Already freighted by material

deprivation, they now had added to their burden the implicit contempt of many above them in the social hierarchy. In such an atmosphere, it seemed rather less fitting for poets to devote their verses to
celebrating the nobility of ploughmen.

Second Story:
Status Does Have Moral Connotations

Central to traditional Christian thought was the claim that status
carried no moral significance. Jesus was the most exalted among
men, but he had been a carpenter. Pilate, who had been an important
imperial official, was a sinner: this incongruence alone proved that a
person's place in the social hierarchy was not reflective of his or her
actual qualities. An intelligent, kind, resourceful, quick and creative
individual might be found sweeping floors, and a chinless, degener-
ate, *fin de race,* sadistic and foolish one governing a nation.

The assertion of a disjuncture between rank and intrinsic value
was hard to refute when in Western societies, positions had for centuries been distributed according to bloodlines and family connections rather than talent, a practice which had resulted in generations
of kings who couldn't rule, lords who couldn't manage their own
estates, commanders who didn't understand the intricacies of battle,
peasants who were brighter than their masters and maids who knew
more than their mistresses.

The pattern held until the middle of the eighteenth century, when
the first voices began to question the hereditary principle. Was it
really wise for fathers always to hand down their businesses to their
sons, without regard to their intelligence? Were the children of roy-
alty necessarily the best suited to run their countries? To highlight
the folly of the principle, comparisons were made with an area of life
where a meritocratic system had long been entrenched and accepted

by even the most committed supporters of hereditary privilege: literature. When it came to choosing a book, what mattered was whether the writing was any good, not whether the author's parents had been famous or wealthy. A talented father did not guarantee literary success, nor an ignominious one failure. Why not, then, import this same objective method of judgement into appointments in political or economic life?

"I smile to myself when I contemplate the ridiculous insignificance into which literature and all the sciences would sink, were they made hereditary, commented Thomas Paine in *The Rights of Man* (1791), and I carry the same idea into governments. A hereditary governor is as inconsistent as an hereditary author. I know not whether Homer or Euclid had sons; but I will venture an opinion that if they had, and had left their works unfinished, those sons could not have completed them."

Napoleon shared Paine's indignation, and early on in his reign, became the first Western leader openly to move towards what he would term a system of *carrières ouvertent aux talents*, "careers open to talent." "I made most of my generals *de la boue*," he proudly recalled on Saint Helena, near the end of his life. "Whenever I found talent, I rewarded it." There was substance to his boast: Napoleonic France witnessed the abolition of feudal privileges and the institution of the Legion of Honour, the first title to be bestowed on individuals of every social rank. The educational system was likewise reformed: *lycées* were opened to all, and in 1794 a polytechnic was founded, offering generous state subsidies to poorer pupils (in its early years, half the students it enrolled were the sons of peasants and artisans). Many of Napoleon's leading appointees came from modest backgrounds, among them his prefects at the Ministry of the Interior, his scientific advisers and a number of senators. In Napoleon's words, hereditary nobles were "the curse of the nation, imbeciles and hereditary asses!"

Even after his fall, Napolean's ideas endured and won over influential proponents in Europe and the United States. Ralph Waldo Emerson expressed a desire to see "every man placed where he belongs, with so much power confided to him as he would carry and use." Thomas Carlyle, for his part, was outraged by the way the children of the rich squandered their money while those of the poor were denied even a rudimentary education: "What shall we say of the Idle Aristocracy, the owners of the soil of England; whose recognised function is that of handsomely consuming the rents of England and shooting the partridges of England?" He railed against those who had never done anything or benefitted anyone, who had not had to prove themselves in any field but had instead been handed their privileges on a plate. He sketched a portrait of the typical English aristocrat, "luxuriously housed up, screened from all work, from want, danger, hardship. He sits serene, amid appliances, and has his work done by other men. And such a man calls himself a *noble*-man? His fathers worked for him, he says; or successfully gambled for him. It is the law of the land, and is thought to be the law of the Universe that this man shall have no task laid on him except that of eating his cooked victuals and not flinging himself out of the window!"

Like many nineteenth-century reformers, Carlyle dreamt not of a world in which everyone would be financially equal, but of one in which high and low alike would come by their inequalities honestly. "Europe requires a real aristocracy," he wrote, "only it must be an aristocracy of talent. False aristocracies are insupportable." What he was imagining was a system whose name had not yet been coined: a meritocracy.

The new ideology of meritocracy competed with two alternative notions of social organization: the egalitarian principle, calling for absolute equality in the distribution of goods among all members of society; and the hereditary principle, endorsing the automatic transfer of titles and posts (and partridge shoots) from the wealthy to their children. Like aristocrats of old, meritocrats were prepared to tolerate a great deal of inequality, but like radical egalitarians, they favoured (if only for a transitional phase) complete equality of opportunity. If everyone received the same education and had the same chance to enter any career, they argued, subsequent differences in income and prestige would be justified by reference to individuals' particular talents and weaknesses. Consequently, there would be no need artificially to equalise salaries or assets; hardships would be merited no less than privileges.

Nineteenth- and twentieth-century social legislation represented the triumph of the meritocratic principle. Equal opportunities were, with varying promptness and differing degrees of sincerity, promoted by the governments of all Western countries. It came to be generally accepted that a decent secondary—and in many cases even a university—education should be made available to every citizen, regardless of income. The United States led the way with the opening, in 1824, of the first truly publicly supported high school. By the time of the Civil War, in the 1860s, there were three hundred such schools, and by 1890, the number stood at twenty-five hundred. In the 1920s, it was the turn of university education to be reformed along meritocratic lines through the introduction of the Scholastic Aptitude Test, or SAT, system. Its founders, the president of Harvard University, James Conant, and the head of the U.S. government's Educational Testing Service, Henry Chauncey, aimed to develop a scientifically proven meritocratic standard by which to assess the intelligence of all applicants in a fair and dispassionate manner, thereby curtailing old-school bias, racism and snobbery in university admissions. Rather than being judged by who their fathers were or how well they were dressed, American pupils would now be ranked according to their real worth—which, in Conant and Chauncey's understanding of the term, meant their ability to solve problems such as the following:

Pick out the antonyms from among these four words:
      obdurate   spurious   ductile   recondite

and:

Say which word, or both or neither, has the same meaning as
the first word:
      impregnable   terile   vacuous
      nominal   exorbitant   didactic

Those who correctly met such challenges could be counted upon to
merit academic success, jobs in Wall Street firms and ensuing membership in country clubs. In Conant's words, the SAT was "a new
type of social instrument whose proper use may be the means of salvation of the classlessness of the nation . . . a means of recapturing
social flexibility, a means of approximating more nearly the American ideal."

This American ideal did not, of course, entail actual equality but
merely an initial period of strictly policed equal opportunity. If all
citizens had the same chance to go to school and find the antonym
among a list of words and enter university, there would be justice in
any aristocracy that ultimately emerged among Americans.

By 1946, the year of the publication of the Universal Declaration
of Human Rights, the promise of its twenty-sixth provision had
become, at least in many parts of Europe and the United States, more
or less a reality: "Everyone has the right to education. Education
shall be free, at least in the elementary and fundamental stages. Elementary education shall be compulsory. Technical and professional
education shall be made generally available and higher education
shall be equally accessible to all on the basis of merit."

Alongside these educational reforms came legislation fostering
equal opportunities in the workplace. In Britain, the landmark

meritocratic measure was the introduction, in 1870, of competitive entrance examinations for the Civil Service. For centuries, the service had been home to the penniless and dim-witted relatives of aristocrats, with some catastrophic results for the empire. By the middle of the nineteenth century, the costs of employing these well-mannered, partridge-shooting fools had grown so high that two government officials, Sir Stafford Northcote and Sir Charles Trevelyan, were asked to devise an alternative system of recruitment. After studying the bureaucracy for a few months, Trevelyan remarked in a letter to the *Times,* "There can be no doubt that our high aristocracy have been accustomed to employ the service as a means of providing for the waifs and strays of their families—as a sort of foundling hospital where those who had no energy to make their way in open professions might receive a nominal office for life at the expense of the public."

Seventy years later, in *The Lion and the Unicorn,* George Orwell was still protesting against the ingrained evils of nepotism. Britain needed a revolution, he insisted, but one without "red flags and street fighting"; instead, what was required was "a fundamental shift of power" towards those who deserved to wield it: "What is wanted is a conscious open revolt by ordinary people against inefficiency, class privilege and the rule of the old. Right through our national life we have got to fight against privilege, against the notion that a half-witted public-schoolboy is better for command than an intelligent mechanic. Although there are gifted and honest *individuals* among them, we have got to break the grip of the moneyed class as a whole. England has got to assume its real shape."

Throughout the developed world, replacing the undeserving with the able became a leading ambition behind employment reform. In the United States, equality of opportunity was pursued with a special intensity. In March 1961, less than two months after assuming office, President John F. Kennedy established a Committee on Equal

Employment Opportunity and charged it with ending employment discrimination in all its forms in government departments and private businesses. A series of specific laws followed: the Equal Pay Act (1963), the Civil Rights Act (1964), the Equal Employment Opportunity Act (1964), the Older Americans Act (1965), the Age Discrimination in Employment Act (1967), the Equal Credit Opportunity Act (1976) and the Americans with Disabilities Act (1990). With such legislation in place, it was plausible to believe, however old one happened to be and whatever one's religion, colour or sex, that one would be guaranteed a fair chance of success.

Although progress towards a purely meritocratic system may have been slow, at times haphazard and as yet incomplete, already from the middle of the nineteenth century, especially in the United States and Britain, the trend had started to influence public perceptions of the relative virtues of the poor and the rich. Once jobs and rewards began to be handed out on the basis of dispassionate interviews and examinations, it could no longer be argued that worldly position was wholly divorced from inner qualities, as many Christian thinkers had proposed, nor could it be claimed that the wealthy and powerful must a priori have attained their station through corrupt means, as Rousseau and Marx had suggested. Once the partridge shooters had been ejected from the Civil Service and replaced with the intelligent offspring of the working classes, once the SATs had emptied Ivy League universities of the witless sons and daughters of East Coast plutocrats and filled them instead with the hardworking children of shop owners, it became harder to maintain that status was the result entirely of a rigged system.

Faith in an increasingly reliable connection between merit and worldly success in turn endowed money with a new moral quality. When riches were still being handed down the generations according to bloodlines and connections, it was natural to dismiss the notion that wealth was an indicator of any virtue besides that of having been born to the right parents. But in a meritocratic world in which prestigious and well-paid jobs could be secured only through native intelligence and ability, money began to look like a sound signifier of character. The rich were not only wealthier, it seemed; they might also be plain *better.*

Over the course of the nineteenth century, many Christian thinkers, particularly in the United States, revised their views on money accordingly. American Protestant denominations preached that God demanded of his followers a life of achievement both temporal and spiritual; the possession of riches in *this* world, it was suggested, was evidence that one deserved a good place in the next, an attitude reflected in the subtitle of the Reverend Thomas P. Hunt's best-seller of 1836, *The Book of Wealth: In Which It Is Proved from the Bible That It Is the Duty of Every Man to Become Rich.* Wealth came to be described as a reward from God for holiness. John D. Rockefeller was unabashed to state that it was the Lord who had made him rich, while William Lawrence, the Episcopal bishop of Massachusetts, writing in 1892, avowed, "In the long run, it is only to the man of morality that wealth comes. We, like the Psalmist, occasionally see the wicked prosper, but only occasionally. Godliness is in league with riches."

Thanks to the meritocratic ideal, multitudes were granted the opportunity to fulfil themselves. Gifted and intelligent individuals of the sort who for centuries had been kept down within an immobile, castelike hierarchy were now free to express their talents on a theoretically level playing field. No longer was background, gender, race or age an impassable obstacle to advancement. An element of justice had finally entered into the distribution of rewards.

But there was also, inevitably, a darker side to the story for those of low status. If the successful merited their success, it necessarily followed that the failures had to merit their failure. In a meritocratic age, an element of justice appeared to enter into the distribution of poverty no less than that of wealth. Low status came to seem not merely regrettable but also *deserved*.

Without doubt, attaining financial success in an economic meritocracy, without the benefit of inheritance or advantages of birth, provided a measure of personal validation that the nobleman of old, who had been given his money and his castle by his father, had never experienced. But at the same time, financial failure became associated with a sense of shame that the peasant of old, denied all chances in life, had also, and more happily, been spared.

The question of why, if one was in any way good, clever or able, one was still poor became more acute and painful for the unsuccessful to have to answer (to themselves and others) in a new meritocratic age.

Third Story:
The Poor Are Sinful and Corrupt
and Owe Their Poverty to Their Own Stupidity

There was no shortage of people willing to answer the question on behalf of the poor during the nineteenth and twentieth centuries. For a certain outspoken constituency, it was clear (and scientifically provable) that the downtrodden had only their own degeneracy and lack of intelligence to blame for their lot in life.

With the rise of the economic meritocracy, the poor moved, in some quarters, from being termed "unfortunate," and seen as the fitting object of the charity and guilt of the rich, to being described as "failures" and regarded as fair targets for the contempt of robust, self-made individuals, who were disinclined to feel ashamed of their mansions or to shed crocodile tears for those whose company they had escaped.

There could have been no more telling expression of the idea of a just distribution of wealth and poverty than the nineteenth-century philosophy of Social Darwinism. Its adherents proposed that all humans began by facing a fair struggle over scarce resources such as money, jobs and esteem. Some gained the upper hand in this contest not because they enjoyed improper advantages or were unfairly lucky but because they were intrinsically *better* than their rivals. The rich were not better, however, from a moral point of view; rather, they were, intimidatingly, *naturally* better: they were more potent, their seed was stronger, their minds were cannier. They were the tigers of the human jungle, predestined by biology—a new, godlike concept before which the nineteenth century genuflected—to outpace others. It was biology that wanted the rich to be rich and the poor to be poor.

The Social Darwinists furthermore insisted that the sufferings and untimely deaths of the poor benefitted society as a whole and should therefore under no circumstances be prevented by government interference. The weak were nature's mistakes and must be allowed to perish before they could reproduce and thereby contaminate the rest of the population. Just as the animal kingdom spawned its share of malformed creatures, so, too, did mankind. The most humane thing was to let the feeble die without misguided mercy.

In his *Social Statics* (1851), the English Social Darwinist Herbert Spencer asserted that biology itself was opposed to charity: "It seems hard that widows and orphans should be left to struggle for life or death. Nevertheless, when regarded not separately, but in connection with the interests of universal humanity, these harsh fatalities are seen to be full of beneficence—the same beneficence which brings to early graves the children of diseased parents. . . . Under the natural order of things society is constantly excreting its unhealthy, imbecile, slow, vacillating, faithless members. If they are sufficiently complete to live, they do live, and it is well that they should live. If they are not sufficiently complete to live, they die, and it is best they should die."

Such doctrines found a receptive audience among the self-made plutocrats who dominated American business and the American media. Social Darwinism provided them with an apparently unassailable scientific argument with which to rebut entities and isms that many of them were already suspicious of, not to mention threatened by on the economic level: trade unions, Marxism and socialism. On a triumphant tour of America in 1882, Spencer was cheered by gatherings of business leaders, who were flattered at being compared to the alpha beasts of the human jungle and relieved to be absolved of any need to feel guilty about or charitable towards their weaker brethren.

Even many who did not expressly adopt a Social Darwinist perspective supported one of the philosophy's key assumptions, agreeing that it was unnecessary and possibly even wrong to provide welfare to the poor. If all had the power to become successful by their own efforts, then political action to assist the lower classes served only to reward failure.

In his book *Self-Help* (1859), the Scottish doctor Samuel Smiles, after encouraging deprived young people to set themselves ambitious goals, get a proper education and be careful with their money, inveighed against any government that might seek to aid them in such pursuits: "Whatever is done *for* men takes away from the stimulus and necessity of doing things for themselves. The value of legislation as an agent in human advancement has been much over-estimated. No laws, however stringent, can make the idle industrious, the thriftless provident or the drunken sober."

The Scottish-American industrial magnate Andrew Carnegie, despite his philanthropy, was at heart similarly pessimistic about the ultimate benefits of welfare: "Of every thousand dollars spent in so-called charity nine hundred and fifty of them had better be thrown into the sea," he remarked in his *Autobiography* (1920). "Every drunken vagabond or lazy idler supported by alms is a source of

*Andrew Carnegie, self-made industrialist
and the world's wealthiest man, 1835–1919*

moral infection to a neighbourhood. It will not do to teach the hard-working, industrious man that there is an easier path by which his wants can be supplied. The less emotion the better. Neither the individual nor the race is improved by alms-giving. Those worthy of assistance, except in rare cases, seldom require assistance. The really valuable men of the race never do."

In the harsher climate of opinion that prevailed in certain strata of meritocratic societies, it now became possible to argue that the social hierarchy rigorously reflected the qualities of those on every rung of the ladder, and that conditions already in place ensured that the worthy would succeed and the undeserving flounder. Any tendency towards charity, welfare, redistributive measures or simple compassion was thus rendered—conveniently—unnecessary.

2.

Michael Young, *The Rise of Meritocracy* (London, 1958):
"Today all persons, however humble, know they have had every chance . . . If they have been labelled 'dunce' repeatedly they cannot any longer pretend. . . . Are they not bound to recognise that they have an inferior status, not as in the past because they were denied opportunity, but because they *are* inferior?"

3.

To the injury of poverty, a meritocratic system now added the insult of shame.

IV
SNOBBERY

1.

Up until a certain age, no one minds much what we do, existence alone is enough to earn us unconditional affection. We can burp up our food, scream at the top of our voice, throw the cutlery on the floor, spend the day gazing blankly out of the window, relieve ourselves in the flower pot—and still know that someone will come and stroke our hair, change our clothes and sing us songs. We begin our time on earth in the hands of a mother, who asks little more of us than that we continue to live. Even those who are not our own mothers, be they men or women, behave as indulgently: they smile when they see us on a family shopping trip, they comment on the pretty patterns of our clothes and, on a lucky day, bring us a furry animal, a few rails of wooden track or a signal box as a reward for just being ourselves.

But this idyllic state is fated not to endure. By the time we have finished our education, we are forced to take our place in a world dominated by a new kind of person, as different from a mother as it is possible to be and whose behaviour lies at the heart of our status anxieties: the snob. Though certain friends and lovers will remain immune from snobbery, will promise not to disown us even if we are bankrupted and disgraced (on a good day, we may even believe them), in general, we are forced to subsist on a diet of the highly conditional attentions of snobs.

2.

The word "snobbery" came into use for the first time in England during the 1820s. It was said to have derived from the habit of many Oxford and Cambridge colleges of writing *sine nobilitate* (without nobility), or "*s.nob*," next to the names of ordinary students on examination lists in order to distinguish them from their aristocratic peers.

In the word's earliest days, a snob was taken to mean someone *without* high status, but it quickly assumed its modern and almost diametrically opposed meaning: someone offended by a lack of high status in *others*, a person who believes in a flawless equation between social rank and human worth. In his *Book of Snobs* (1848), a pioneering essay on the subject, William Thackeray observed that over the previous twenty-five years, snobs had "spread over England like the railroads. They are now known and recognized throughout an Empire on which the sun never sets."

Though traditionally they may have been associated with an interest in the aristocracy (for they were first pinned down in language at a time and place when aristocrats stood at the social apex), the identification of snobbery with an enthusiasm for old-world manners, blazers, hunting and gentlemen's clubs hardly captures the diversity of the phenomenon. It lets too many off the hook. Snobs can be found through history ingratiating themselves with a range of prominent groups—from soldiers (Sparta, 400 B.C.), bishops (Rome, 1500), and poets (Weimar, 1815), to farmers (China, 1967), and film stars (Hollywood, 2004)—for the primary interest of snobs is power, and as the distribution of power changes, so, naturally and immediately, will the objects of their admiration.

3.

It is easy to recognise the moment when we have entered the orbit of a snob. Early on in an encounter, the subject of what we "do" will arise and depending on how we answer, we will either be the recipients of bountiful attention or the catalysts of urgent disgust.

The company of the snobbish has the power to enrage and unnerve because we sense how little of who we are deep down—that is, how little of who we are outside of our status—will be able to govern their behaviour towards us. We may be endowed with the wisdom of Solomon and have the resourcefulness and intelligence of Odysseus, but if we are unable to wield socially recognized badges of our qualities, our existence will remain a matter of raw indifference to them.

This conditional attention pains us because our earliest memory of love is of being cared for in a naked, impoverished condition. Babies cannot, by definition, repay their caretakers with worldly rewards. In so far as they are loved and looked after, it is therefore for who they are, identity understood in its barest, most stripped-down state. They are loved for, or in spite of, their uncontrolled, howling and stubborn characters.

Only as we mature does affection begin to depend on achievement: being polite, succeeding at school and later, acquiring rank and prestige. Such efforts may attract the interest of others, but the underlying emotional craving is not so much to dazzle because of our deeds as to recapture the tenor of the bountiful, indiscriminate petting we received in return for arranging wooden bricks on the kitchen floor, for having a soft plump body and wide trusting eyes.

It is evidence of this craving that only the most inept flatterer would admit to a wish to base a friendship around an attraction to power or fame. Such assets would feel like insulting and volatile reasons to be invited to lunch, for they lie outside the circle of our true and irreducible selves. Jobs can be lost and influence eroded without us perishing nor our childhood-founded need for affection slackening. Talented flatterers therefore know they should suggest that it is strictly the status-less part of their prey they are interested in, that the ambassadorial car, newspaper profiles or company directorship are mere coincidental features of a profound and pure attachment.

Yet, despite their efforts, the prey are liable to detect the fickleness beneath the polished surface and leave the company of snobs fearing the irrelevance of their essential selves beside any status which, for a time, they may hold precariously in their hands.

4.

Given their exclusive interest in reputation and achievement, snobs are prone to make some sudden tragi-comic reassessments of who their closest friends might be when the outer circumstances of their acquaintances alter.

On a foggy evening in Paris at the end of the nineteenth century, the bourgeois narrator of Marcel Proust's *In Search of Lost Time* (1922) travels to an expensive restaurant to have dinner with an aristocratic friend, the Marquis de Saint-Loup. He arrives early, Saint-Loup is late and the staff, judging their client on the basis of a shabby coat and an unfamiliar name, assume that a nobody has entered their establishment. They therefore patronize him, take him to a table around which an arctic draught is blowing and are slow to offer him anything to drink or eat.

But, a quarter of an hour later, the marquis arrives, identifies his friend and at a stroke transforms the narrator's value in the eyes of the staff. The manager bows deeply before him, draws out the menu, recites the specials of the day with evocative flourishes, compliments him on his clothes and, so as to prevent him thinking that these courtesies are in any way dependent on his link to an aristocrat, occasionally gives him a surreptitious little smile that seems to indicate a wholly personal affection. When the narrator asks him for some bread, the manager clicks his heels and exclaims:

"Certainly, Monsieur le baron!" "I am not a baron," I told him in a tone of mock sadness. "Oh, I beg your pardon, Monsieur le comte!" I had no time to lodge a second protest, which would no doubt have promoted me to the rank of marquis.

However satisfactory the volte-face, the underlying dynamic is bleak, for the manager has not of course amended his snobbish value system in any way. He has merely rewarded someone differently within its brutal confines—and only rarely do we have the opportunity to find a Marquis de Saint-Loup or a Prince Charming who will speak up on our behalf to convince the world of the nobility of our souls. More commonly, we are made to finish our dinner in the arctic draught.

5.

The problem is compounded by newspapers. Because snobs combine a weak capacity for independent judgement with an appetite for the views of influential people, their beliefs will, to a critical degree, be set by the atmosphere of the press.

Thackeray proposed that the obsessive English concern with high status and the aristocracy could be traced back to the country's papers, which daily reinforced messages about the prestige of the titled and the famous and, by implication, the banality of the untitled and the ordinary. His particular bugbear was the "Court Circular" section of the papers, which reverently covered the parties, holidays, births and deaths of "high society." In October 1848 (the month of publication of his *Book of Snobs*), the Court Circular of the *Morning Post* reported on Lord Brougham's hunting party at Brougham Hall ("a good sport was had by all"), Lady Agnes Duff's impending accouchement in Edinburgh and Georgina Pakenham's marriage to Lord Burghley ("Her Ladyship was magnificently attired in a white satin dress, with lace flounces and a corsage montant. It is needless to say that she looked exquisite").

"How can you help being snobs, so long as this balderdash is set before you?" demanded Thackeray. "Oh, down with the papers, those engines and propagators of snobbishness!" And, to expand on Thackeray's thought, how greatly the levels of status anxiety of the population might diminish if only our own newspapers were to exchange a fraction of their interest in Lady Agnes Duff and her successors for a focus on the significance of ordinary life.

6.

It is perhaps only ever fear that is to blame. Belittling others is no pastime for those convinced of their own standing. There is terror behind haughtiness. It takes a punishing impression of our own inferiority to leave others feeling that they aren't good enough for us.

The fear flows down the generations. In a pattern common to all abusive behaviour, snobs generate snobs. An older generation inflicts its own unusually powerful association between modest rank and catastrophe, denying its offspring the layer of emotional bedding that would grant them the inner ease to imagine that low status (their own and that of others) does not neatly equate with unworthiness, nor high status with excellence.

"There go the Spicer Wilcoxes, Mamma!" a daughter exclaims to her mother while walking in Hyde Park on a spring morning in a *Punch* cartoon of 1892. "I'm told they're dying to know us. Hadn't we better call?"

"Certainly not, Dear," replies the mother, labouring under an ancestral sense of unworthiness. "If they're dying to know us, they're not worth knowing. The only People worth *Our* knowing are the people who don't want to know us!"

Unless Mamma can be helped to heal the scars to which her behaviour testifies, there is little hope that she will ever be capable of a more rounded interest in the Spicer Wilcoxes—and so little hope that the cycles of fear-induced snobbery will ever be interrupted.

Yet it is hard to renounce snobbish tactics on our own, for the disease is a collective one to begin with. A youthful resentment of snobbery isn't enough to save us from gradually turning into snobs

"THERE GO THE SPICER WILCOXES, MAMMA! I'M TOLD THEY'RE DYING TO KNOW US. HADN'T WE BETTER CALL?"
"CERTAINLY NOT, DEAR. IF THEY'RE DYING TO KNOW US, THEY'RE NOT WORTH KNOWING. THE ONLY PEOPLE WORTH *OUR*
KNOWING ARE THE PEOPLE WHO DON'T WANT TO KNOW US!"

Illustration from Punch, *1892*

ourselves, because being insolently neglected almost naturally fosters a hunger to gain the attention of our neglectors (disliking people rarely being a sufficient reason for not wanting *them* to like *us*). The snobbery of a prominent group can thereby draw the population as a whole towards social ambitions that it may initially have had no taste for but now pursues as the only apparent means to love and recognition. Rather than scorn, sorrow and understanding might be more accurate responses to behaviour motivated at heart by a frightened and frustrated desire for dignity.

It may be tempting to laugh at those afflicted by urgent cravings for the symbols of status. The name-droppers, the gold-tap owners. The history of Victorian furniture, for example, was dominated by the sale of some candidly tasteless items. Many of them were the work of the London firm of Jackson & Graham, whose most flamboyant offering was a carved cabinet of pollard oak, decked out with figures of boys gathering grapes, two female caryatids and a set of carved pilasters. The whole was crowned by a majestic sixty-centimetre-high gold-plated bull.

Before ridiculing anyone who bought such a piece, it would perhaps be fairer to wonder about the wider context in which this kind of furniture was made and consumed. Rather than teasing the buyers, we may blame the society in which they lived for setting up a situation where the purchase of ornate cabinets felt psychologically necessary and rewarding, where respect was dependent on baroque displays. Rather than a tale of greed, the history of luxury could more accurately be read as a record of emotional trauma. It is the legacy of those who have felt pressured by the disdain of others to add an extraordinary amount to their bare selves in order to signal that they too may lay a claim to love.

7.

If poverty is the customary material penalty for low status, then neglect and faraway looks are the emotional penalties that a snobbish world appears unable to stop imposing on those bereft of the symbols of importance.

Carved cabinet of pollard oak, Jackson & Graham, London, 1852

V

DEPENDENCE

Factors of Dependence

1.

In traditional societies, high status may have been inordinately hard to acquire, but it was also comfortingly hard to lose. It was as difficult to stop being a lord as, more darkly, it was to cease being a peasant. What mattered was one's identity at birth, rather than anything one might achieve in one's lifetime through the exercise of one's faculties. What mattered was who one was, seldom what one did.

The great aspiration of modern societies has been to reverse this equation, to strip away both inherited privilege and inherited underprivilege in order to make rank dependent on individual achievement—which has come primarily to mean financial achievement. Status now rarely depends on an unchangeable identity handed down the generations; rather, it hangs on performance in a fastmoving and implacable economy.

It is in the nature of this economy that the most evident trait of the struggle to achieve status should be uncertainty. We contemplate the future in the knowledge that we may at any time be thwarted by colleagues or competitors, or discover that we lack the talents to reach our chosen goals, or steer into an inauspicious current in the swells of the marketplace—any failure being compounded by the possible success of our peers.

Anxiety is the handmaiden of contemporary ambition, for our livelihoods and esteem rest on at least five unpredictable elements, offering us five good reasons never to count on either attaining or holding on to our desired position within the hierarchy.

1. Dependence on Fickle Talent

If our status depends on our achievements, then what we may need most in order to succeed is talent and, where peace of mind is a priority, reliable control over it. In most activities, however, talent is impossible to direct as we please. It can make an appearance for a time and then unapologetically vanish, leaving our career in pieces. We cannot call the best of ourselves to the fore at will. So far are we from owning what talent we do on occasion display, that our achievements can seem like a gift granted to us by an external agency, a gift upon whose erratic presence and absence hang not only our ability to pay for the objects around us but the very course of our lives.

It was the ancient Greeks who came up with the most acute image to evoke our distressingly volatile relationship with talent, when they named the Muses. According to Greek mythology, each of these nine demideities held sway over, and fitfully bestowed on chosen souls, a particular ability: in epic poetry, history, love poetry, music, tragedy, the writing of hymns, dancing, comedy or astronomy. Those who experienced success in any of these fields were reminded that their gifts were never truly their own and might be spirited away again at a stroke if the thin-skinned givers changed their minds.

The areas in which the Greek Muses were said to operate hardly reflect contemporary concerns. And yet the mythological idiom continues to capture something meaningful about the weak hold we have upon our own powers to achieve, and about the subservient, anxious position we are thereby compelled to adopt in relation to our future.

2. Dependence on Luck

Our status also depends on a range of favourable conditions that could be loosely defined by the word *luck*. It may be merely good luck that places us in the right occupation, with the right skills, at the right time, and little more than bad luck that denies us the selfsame advantages.

But pointing to luck as an explanation for what happens in our lives has, regrettably, become effectively unacceptable. In less technologically sophisticated eras, when mankind respected the power of the gods and the unpredictable moods of nature, the idea of our having no control over events had wide currency. Gratitude and blame were routinely laid on the doorstep of external agencies, with reference made to the intervention of demons, goblins, spirits and gods. Throughout the story of *Beowulf* (circa A.D. 1100), for example, we are told that the success of man depends on the will of the Christian God; describing his defeat of Grendel's mother, Beowulf himself asserts that "the fight would have ended straightaway if God had not guarded me."

As our power to control and anticipate the behaviour of our environment has increased, however, so has the concept of luck or of guardian deities lost its potency. While few would deny outright that luck retains a theoretical role in mapping the course of careers, the evaluation of individuals proceeds, in practical terms, on the assumption that they may fairly be held responsible for their own biographies. It would sound to our ears unduly (and even suspiciously) modest for someone to ascribe a personal or professional triumph to "good luck," and more significantly in this context, pitiable to blame defeat on the opposite. Winners make their own luck, so goes the modern mantra—an aphorism that would have puzzled the ancient Roman worshippers of the goddess of fortune or the faithful heroes of *Beowulf.*

It is alarming enough to have to rely for one's status on contingent elements. It is harder yet to live in a world so enamoured with notions of rational control that it has largely dismissed "bad luck" as a credible explanation for defeat.

3. Dependence on an Employer

The unpredictability of our condition is further aggravated by the likelihood that our status will be bound up with the priorities of an employer.

In the United States in 1907, a book entitled *Three Acres and Liberty* seized the imagination of the reading public. The author, Bolton Hall, began by taking for granted the awkwardness of having to work for someone else, and so advised his readers that they could win their freedom by leaving their offices and factories and buying three acres apiece of inexpensive farmland in middle America. This acreage would soon enable them to grow enough food for a family of four and to build a simple but comfortable home, and best of all, relieve them of any need ever again to flatter or negotiate with colleagues and superiors. The balance of the book was given over to detailed descriptions of how to plant vegetables, construct a greenhouse, lay out an orchard and buy farm animals (one cow was sufficient for milk and cheese, explained Hall, and ducks made for more nutritious eating than chickens). The message delivered by *Three Acres and Liberty* had been heard with growing frequency over the previous fifty years in both Europe and America: in order to lead a happy life, one must attempt to escape reliance on employers and instead work directly for oneself, at one's own pace, for one's own rewards.

Such calls had come in response to an opposing trend: during the nineteenth century, for the first time in history, a majority of people ceased working on their own farms or in small family businesses and began bartering their intelligence or their strength for a wage paid them by someone else. In 1800, just 20 percent of American workers had an employer other than themselves; by 1900, the figure was up to 50 percent, and by 2000, 90 percent. Employers were also getting larger: whereas in 1800, less than 1 percent of the American workforce was employed in an organisation having five hundred or more employees, by 2000, the figure stood at 55 percent.

In England, the transition from a nation of small agricultural producers to one of wage earners was accelerated by the loss of much commonly owned land, a resource which had enabled the rural poor to survive by growing food for themselves and letting their livestock—a cow or a goose—roam free to graze or forage. From the eighteenth century onwards, the majority of "open" English fields were enclosed behind walls and hedges by powerful landowners. Between 1724 and 1815, more than a million and a half acres of land were privatised. According to traditional Marxist analysis (strongly challenged by historians but revealing nonetheless), the enclosure movement heralded the birth of a modern industrial proletariat, defined as a group of people unable to be self-sufficient and hence left with no option but to sell themselves to an employer at a rate and under conditions heavily weighted in the employer's favour.

Now as then, the travails of being an employee include not only worry over the duration of one's employment but also the everyday humiliation of many working practises and dynamics. Because most businesses are shaped like pyramids, with a wide base of employees giving way to a narrow tip of managers, the question of who will be promoted, and who left behind, typically becomes one of the most oppressive anxieties of the workplace—and one that, like all anxieties, feeds off uncertainty. Compounding the misery is the fact that because achievement in most fields is difficult to monitor reliably, the path to promotion or its opposite may have an apparently haphazard relationship to performance. The successful alpinists of organisational pyramids may not be the employees who are best at their tasks, but those who have best mastered a range of political skills in which ordinary life does not generally offer instruction.

Despite the surface differences between modern businesses and royal courts, perhaps the most penetrating advice on the requirements for survival in the former was provided by a succession of clear-eyed noblemen who lived in the latter in France and Italy between the fifteenth and seventeenth centuries. In retirement, these men collected their thoughts in a series of cynical works written in a tart, aphoristic style—works that continue even today to test the limits of what we would like to believe about our fellow human beings. The observations of Machiavelli (1469–1527), Guicciardini (1483–1540), La Rochefoucauld (1613–1680) and La Bruyère (1645–1696) give a prescient indication of the manoeuvres that workers may, outside their regularly advertised roles, have to execute if they wish to flourish.

On the need to beware of colleagues:

Men are so false, so insidious, so deceitful and cunning in their wiles, so avid in their own interest, and so oblivious to others' interests, that you cannot go wrong if you believe little and trust less.

GUICCIARDINI

We must live with our enemies as if they might one day become our friends, and live with our friends as if they might sometime or other become our enemies.

LA BRUYÈRE

On the need to lie and exaggerate:

The world more often rewards outward signs of merit than merit itself.

LA ROCHEFOUCAULD

If you are involved in important affairs . . . , you must always hide your failures and exaggerate your successes. It is a form of swindling, but since your fate more often depends upon the opinion of others rather than on facts, it is a good idea to create the impression that things are going well.

GUICCIARDINI

You are an honest man, and do not make it your business either to please or to displease the favourites. You are merely attached to your master and to your duty. You are finished.

LA BRUYÈRE

On the need to threaten:

It is much safer to be feared than loved. Love is sustained by a bond of gratitude which, because men are excessively self-interested, is broken whenever they see a chance to benefit themselves. But fear is sustained by a dread of punishment that is always effective.

MACHIAVELLI

Since the majority of men are either not very good or not very wise, one must rely more on severity than on kindness.

GUICCIARDINI

It may, of course, be possible to acquire the velvet glove and iron fist of a courtier, and possible, too, to learn to navigate around colleagues as we might around a reef-ringed coastline—but having the need to do so is scarcely calming. From the perspective of an office or a factory floor, it is easy to fathom the lure of three acres, half a dozen ducks and liberty.

4. *Dependence on an Employer's Profitability*

For a worker in an organisation, job security depends not only on internal politics but also, and more ominously, on the company's ability to remain profitable in a marketplace in which few producers can defend their competitive position or pricing power for long. If the ferocity of the competition inflicts on many workforces an anxiety not dissimilar to that one might feel when standing on a melting ice floe, it is perhaps because the most effective and swiftest way for management to improve profitability is almost always to decimate staffing levels.

Companies under financial pressure may find it hard to resist dispensing with workers in countries where wages are high in order to hire cheaper replacements in faraway lands. They may equally be tempted to enhance profitability by merging with competitors, in the process eliminating great swathes of duplicate workforces. Or again, they may turn to mechanisation, computers or robots. Consider, for example, the automatic teller machine, or ATM, which was developed in 1968 and first unveiled the following year, when a single unit was fitted into a hole in the wall at a branch of Manhattan's Chemical Bank. Within a decade, 50,000 ATMs were in operation worldwide; by 2000, the number had risen to 1,000,000. But however technologically impressive they were, ATMs offered flesh-and-blood bank tellers few grounds for celebration: studies soon showed that one ATM could do the work of no fewer than thirty-seven human tellers (and, into the bargain, rarely fell ill). In the United States, about half of all those employed in retail banking—some 500,000 people—lost their jobs between 1980 and 1995, thanks in large part to the invention of these silkily efficient machines.

As if all that weren't troubling enough, employees must in addition worry about the consequences of the pressure put on companies to introduce new and better products into the marketplace. For long stretches of history, the life cycles of goods and services exceeded those of the human beings who produced and consumed them. In Japan, the kimono and jinbaori went unchanged for four hundred years. In China, people were still wearing in the eighteenth century exactly what their ancestors had worn in the sixteenth. Between 1300 and 1660, plough design did not alter across northern Europe. Such stability of production must have given artisans and labourers a reassuring sense that their work would outlive them. Since the middle of the nineteenth century, however, product life cycles have been sharply attenuated, and the trend has shaken workers' confidence in the long-term integrity of their careers.

Sudden and decisive trouncings of old products and services by new ones have occurred in almost every area of the economy, as canals were made obsolete by the invention of the railway, passenger liners by the introduction of the jet engine, horses by the development of the car and typewriters by the proliferation of the personal computer.

The market's passion for movement and change can burden companies with product-development costs so enormous that their very survival must depend on the successful launch of a single item. Like a palpitating high roller who, instead of being allowed to cash in his winnings after a good run, is forced at gunpoint to continue risking his assets, a corporation may have to let everything ride on the outcome of a few wagers or even a solitary bet, and as a result either amass vast but precarious riches, or, alternatively, self-destruct.

5. *Dependence on the Global Economy*

The survival of both companies and their employees is further threatened by the performance of the economy as a whole.

The history of the economies of Western nations has, since the early nineteenth century, been one of repeated cycles of growth and recession. Typically, four or five years of expansion have been followed by one or two of retraction, with occasional massive retrenchments lasting five or six years. Graphs of national wealth often resemble the profiles of angular mountain ranges, in whose every valley lie the bankruptcies of long-established firms, the layoffs of workforces, the closings of factories, the destruction of stock. We may seek to attribute these events to unnatural dimensions of economic life, and we may hope that one day we will learn to avert them, but for the time being, the best efforts of governments and central banks have demonstrated that there is little to be done about such turbulence.

Every cycle follows a similar pattern. It begins when growth picks up and companies invest in new capacity to meet perceived future needs. Production costs tend to escalate at this stage, as do asset prices, especially for equities and property, driven up in part by speculators. Inexpensive credit encourages businesses to commit to large, capital-intensive factories and offices. At this critical point, demand and current output both begin to slow, even as consumption continues to accelerate. A lack of savings spurs an increase in personal and commercial borrowing. To satisfy domestic demand, companies start to import more and export less, a trend that soon results in a balance-of-payments deficit. The economy is now officially out of kilter, freighted by overinvesting, overconsumption, overborrowing and overlending. Here begins the slide into recession. Prices are pushed higher by the use of less efficient means of production, by the growth in the money supply and by speculation. Tighter and much more expensive credit raises the cost of outstanding debt. Asset values, inflated in the upswing, are punctured. Borrowers can no longer make their payments, and the collateral available for new loans is restricted. Incomes, investment and consumption all fall off.

Companies and entrepreneurs flounder or go bankrupt; unemployment rates rise. As confidence evaporates, borrowing and spending dry up. Long-term capital investments made in better days now come on line, increasing supply and depressing prices just as demand is slackening. Companies and individuals are forced to sell off assets at a loss, deepening the crisis, but many potential buyers wait for the market to hit bottom before purchasing, further delaying recovery.

Rather than a sign of hysteria, a state of steady anxiety may be a reasonable response to the very real threats of the economic environment.

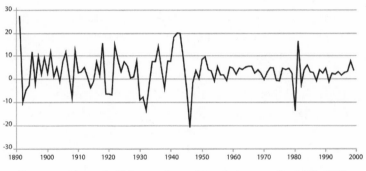

Percentage change in U.S. gross domestic product per capita, 1890–2000

2.

If we are anguished by the thought of failure, it may be because success seems the only dependable incentive for the world to grant us its goodwill. A family bond, a friendship or a sexual attraction may at times render material incentives unnecessary, but only a reckless optimist would rely on emotional currencies for the regular fulfilment of his or her needs. Humans rarely smile without having some robust reason to do so.

3.

Adam Smith, *The Wealth of Nations* (Edinburgh, 1776):
"Man has almost constant occasion for the help of his brethren. [However], it is in vain for him to expect this from their benevolence only. He will be more likely to prevail if he can interest their self-love. . . . It is not from the benevolence of the butcher, the brewer or the baker that we expect our dinner, but from their regard to their own interest. We address ourselves not to their humanity, but to their self-love."

4.

According to one thesis, butchers, brewers and bakers were not always so ruthless. They may once have put food and drink before a man not because he was able to offer them payment in return, but because he had a pleasant manner or was an acquaintance of a distant relative. Financial self-interest has not, this theory holds, forever enjoyed exclusive rule; rather, it is a relatively recent historical development, a product of the modern age and of advanced capitalism. In the feudal age, this thesis goes on, such self-interest was well counterbalanced by nonmaterial considerations. Workers were thought of as members of their employers' extended families and commanded a fitting measure of loyalty and gratitude. Christian teachings helped to foster a general concern for the vulnerable and the hungry, promoting a tacit understanding that in difficult times, they should be cared for.

But such patriarchal, communal relationships were, this selfsame thesis alleges, destroyed by the bourgeoisie's ascent to power in the second half of the eighteenth century. The bourgeois class, hugely powerful through its tight grip on capital and technology, was interested only in wealth. Unsentimental and utilitarian, it viewed employees as nothing more than a means to its acquisitive ends; it cared little for their families and refused to be dictated to by the needs of the sick or the old or the wide-eyed young. At the same time, populations were gravitating towards the larger cities, where neighbourly care was trampled by the competitive, hurried atmosphere of the marketplace. Adding to the woes of the underclass was that Christianity had lost its grip on the imagination of those holding the levers of power, and with it all influence over their treatment of the poor and their sense of community.

In *The Communist Manifesto,* Karl Marx, the most forceful proponent of this thesis, described the triumph of financial concerns in visionary and apocalyptic prose: "The bourgeoisie has . . . pitilessly torn asunder the motley feudal ties that bound man to his 'natural superiors' and has left remaining no other nexus between man and man than naked self-interest, than callous 'cash payment.' It has drowned the most heavenly ecstasies of religious fervour, of chivalrous enthusiasm, of philistine sentimentalism, in the icy water of egotistical calculation. It has resolved personal worth into exchange value."

In his *Groundwork of the Metaphysic of Morals* (1785), Immanuel Kant had argued that behaving morally towards others required one to respect them "for themselves" and not use them as a "means" to one's own enrichment or glory. With reference to Kant, Marx now accused the bourgeoisie, and its new science of economics, of practising "immorality" on a grand scale: "[Economics] knows the worker only as a working animal—as a beast reduced to strictest bodily needs," he charged in the *Manifesto.* The wages paid to workers were, he believed, just "like the oil which is applied to wheels to keep them turning . . . The true purpose of work is no longer man, but money."

5.

Marx may have been a poor historian, erratically idealizing the preindustrial past and unduly castigating the bourgeoisie, but his theories are of value for capturing and dramatising an inescapable degree of conflict between employer and employee.

Beneath the many regional variations and differences evident in style and management, the rationale for almost all commercial organisations can be broken down into a simple and arid equation:

INPUT   OUTPUT

Raw Materials + Labour + Machinery = Product + Profit

To maximise output, every organisation will strive to obtain its necessary raw materials, labour and machinery at the lowest possible cost and combine them to turn out a product that it will then attempt to sell at the highest possible price. From a purely economic perspective, there is no distinction to be made among any of the elements on the input side of the equation. All are commodities that the rational executive will seek to source cheaply and handle efficiently in pursuit of profit.

And yet, troublingly, there *is* one difference between "labour" and other commodities, a difference that conventional economics does not have a means of representing or giving weight to but that is nevertheless unavoidably present in the world: that labour feels pain.

If production lines grow prohibitively expensive, they may be switched off and will not cry at the seeming injustice of their fate. A business can move from using coal to using natural gas without the neglected energy source jumping off a cliff. Labour, by contrast, has a habit of reacting emotionally to any attempt to reduce its price or its presence. It sobs in toilet cubicles, it drinks to ease its fears of underachievement and it may choose death over redundancy.

Such emotive responses alert us to two divergent imperatives that coexist within the arena in which status is accorded: the *economic imperative,* which dictates that the primary task of business is to realize a profit; and the *human imperative,* which causes employees to hunger for financial security, respect and tenure.

While these imperatives may for long periods coincide without apparent friction, all but the most deluded of wage-dependent workers knows for a certainty that whenever a company is faced with making a serious choice between the two, it is the economic imperative that will always, by the very logic of the commercial system, win out.

Struggles between labour and capital may no longer—in the developed world, at least—be as bare-knuckled as they were in Marx's day. Yet despite improvements in working conditions and advances in employment legislation, workers de facto remain tools in a production process to which their own happiness and economic welfare are incidental. Whatever camaraderie may be nurtured between employers and employees, whatever goodwill the latter may display towards the former and however many years they may have devoted to a job or task, workers must live with the anxiety of knowing that their status will never be guaranteed but will be forever dependent on both their own performance and the economic well-being of their organisations. They must accept that they are only a means to an end and not, much as they might long to be so on an emotional level, an end in themselves.

6.

Although the fear of being left penniless is a primary reason for our worry over the instability of our employment, it is not the only reason. We also worry—and here we return to our earliest theme—because of love, for our work is the chief determinant of the amount of respect and care we will be granted. It is according to how we are able to answer the question of what we *do* (normally the first enquiry we will have to field in any new acquaintance) that the quality of our reception is likely to be decided.

Unfortunately for our mental health, our capacity to provide a sufficiently elevated answer to the query rarely lies securely in our own province. It depends instead on the peaks and troughs of the economists' graphs, on struggles in the marketplace and on the vagaries of luck and of inspiration. Meanwhile, for its part, our need for love remains unwavering, no less steady or insistent than it may have been when we were infants, an imbalance between our requirements and the uncertain conditions of the world that constitutes a stubborn fifth pillar on which our status anxieties rest.

PART TWO

SOLUTIONS

I
PHILOSOPHY

Honour and Vulnerability

1.

In Hamburg in 1834, a handsome young army officer named Baron von Trautmansdorf challenged a fellow officer, Baron von Ropp, to a duel. The precipitating offense was a poem that von Ropp had written and circulated among his friends about von Trautmansdorf's moustache, stating that it was thin and floppy and hinting that it might not be the only part of his physique to which those adjectives could be applied. The feud between the barons had originated in their shared passion for the same woman, Countess Lodoiska, the grey-green-eyed widow of a Polish general. Unable to resolve their differences amicably, the two men met in a field in a Hamburg suburb early on a March morning. Both were carrying swords; both were still short of their thirtieth birthdays; both would die in the ensuing fight.

In this last aspect, the event was no exception. From its beginnings in Renaissance Italy until its end in the First World War, the practice of duelling claimed the lives of hundreds of thousands of Europeans. In the seventeenth century, duels were responsible for some five thousand deaths in Spain alone. Visitors to that country were advised to take extra care when addressing the locals, lest they accidentally offend their honour and end up in the grave. "Duels happen every day in Spain," declares a character in a play by Calderón. In France, meanwhile, Lord Herbert of Cherbury reported in 1608 that there was "scarce any man thought worth the looking on, that had not killed some other in a duel," and in England, it was widely held that no man could be termed a gentleman unless and until he had "taken up his sword."

Although occasional duels were sparked by matters of objective importance, the majority had their origin in small, even petty, questions of honour. In Paris in 1678, for example, one man killed another who had said his apartment was tasteless. In Florence in 1702, a literary man took the life of a cousin who had accused him of not understanding Dante. And in France under the regency of Philippe d'Orléans, two officers of the guard fought on the Quai des Tuileries over the ownership of an Angora cat.

2.

For as long as it lasted, duelling symbolised a radical incapacity to believe that one's status might be one's own business, a value one decided on and did not revise to accord with the shifting judgements of others. In the dueller's psyche, other people's opinions were the *only* factor in forming a sense of self. The dueller could not remain acceptable in his own eyes if those around him judged him to be evil or dishonourable, a coward or a failure, foolish or effeminate. So dependent was his self-image on the views of others that he would sooner die of a bullet or stab wound than allow unfavourable assessments of him to go unanswered.

Entire societies have made the maintenance of status, and more particularly of "honour," a primary task of every adult male. Whether called, as in traditional Greek village society, *tīmē*, as in Muslim communities, *sharaf*, or as among Hindus, *izzat*, honour was expected in all cases to be upheld through violence. In traditional Spanish communities, to be worthy of *honra*, a man had to be physically brave, sexually potent, predatory towards women before he was married and loyal thereafter, able to look after his family financially and authoritative enough towards his wife to ensure that she did not have sex or even engage in flirtatious banter with other men. Dishonour was the penalty not only for infringing on codes oneself but also for failing to respond with appropriate fury to an *injuria* inflicted by another. If one was ridiculed in the market square or given an offensive look in the street, doing anything short of soliciting a fight would only confirm the offenders' point.

3.

While we may look askance at those who resort to violence to answer questions of honour, we are nevertheless liable ourselves to share the most significant aspect of their mind-set—that is, an extreme vulnerability to the disdain of others. Like the most hotheaded of duellers, we are likely to base our self-esteem on the value we are commonly accorded. Duelling is merely a helpfully far-fetched historical example of the more universal but equally thin-skinned emotional disposition that almost all of us exhibit in matters of status.

The intense need to be viewed favourably by others may still be foremost among our priorities. The fear of becoming what the Spanish termed a *deshonrado,* or "dishonoured one"—a category whose contemporary connotations might best be captured by the chillingly contemptuous word *loser*—may today be no less haunting than it was for the characters in Calderón's and Lope de Vega's tragedies. Being denied status—for example, because one has failed to reach certain professional goals or is unable to provide for one's family—may be as painful for a modern Westerner as a loss of *honra, tīmē, sharaf* or *izzat* was for a member of a seemingly more hidebound society.

Philosophy and Invulnerability

Other people's heads are too wretched a place for true happiness to have its seat.

SCHOPENHAUER, *PARERGA AND PARALIPOMENA* (1851)

Nature didn't tell me: "Don't be poor." Nor indeed: "Be rich." But she does beg me: "Be independent."

CHAMFORT, *MAXIMS* (1795)

It is not my place in society that makes me well off, but my judgements, and these I can carry with me . . . These alone are my own and cannot be taken away.

EPICTETUS, *DISCOURSES* (CIRCA A.D. 100)

1.

On the Greek peninsula, early in the fifth century B.C., there emerged a group of individuals, many of them bearded, who were singularly free of the anxieties over status that tormented their contemporaries. Untroubled by either the psychological or the material consequences attendant on a humble position in society, these men remained calm in the face of insult, disapproval and penury. When Socrates, for example, saw a pile of gold and jewellery being borne in procession through the streets of Athens, he exclaimed, "Look how many things there are which I don't want." As Alexander the Great was passing through Corinth, he sought out Diogenes and finally found him sitting under a tree, dressed in rags, with not a drachma to his name. When the most powerful man in the world asked the philosopher if he could do anything to help him, Diogenes replied, "Yes, if you could step out of the way. You are blocking the sun." Alexander's sol-

diers were horrified and steeled themselves for the inevitable outburst of their commander's famous anger. But he only laughed and
remarked that if he were not Alexander, he would certainly like to be
Diogenes. Antisthenes, for his part, when informed that a great
many people in Athens had started to praise him, demanded, "Why,
what have I done wrong?" Empedocles evinced a similar scepticism
regarding the intelligence of others. He once lit a lamp in broad day-
light and announced, as he went around, "I am looking for someone
with a mind." And Socrates again, on being insulted in the marketplace, asked by a passerby, "Don't you worry about being called
names?" retorted, "Why? Do you think I should resent it if an ass had
kicked me?"

2.

These philosophers had not ceased to draw distinction between
kindness and ridicule, success and failure; rather, they had settled on
a way of responding to the darker half of the equation that owed
nothing to the traditional honour code. They implicitly refuted its
suggestion that what others think of us must determine what we
may think of ourselves, and that every insult, whether accurate or
not, must shame us.

OTHERS' VIEW   SELF-IMAGE
You are dishonourable ⟶ I am dishonourable

Philosophy introduced a new, mediating element into the relationship between internal and external opinion. This might be visu-
alised as a box in which all public perceptions of a person, whether
positive or negative, would first be deposited in order to be assessed,
thence to be either sent on to the self with renewed force (if they

were true) or else (if they were false) ejected harmlessly into the atmosphere, dispersed with a laugh or a shrug of the shoulders. The philosophers termed the box "reason."

OTHERS' VIEW   SELF-IMAGE

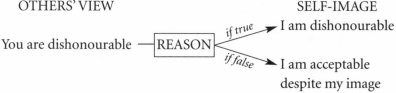

According to the rules of reason, a given conclusion should be deemed true if, and only if, it flows from a logical sequence of thoughts founded on sound initial premises. Taking mathematics as the model of good thinking, philosophers began to search for an approximation of that discipline's objective certainties within the context of ethical life. Thanks to reason, one's status could—these thinkers proposed—be fixed through the agency of an intellectual conscience, instead of being abandoned to the whims and emotions of the market square. If rational examination revealed that one had been unfairly treated by the community, one should be no more perturbed by the judgement than by the ranting, say, of a deluded stranger bent on proving that two and two amounted to five.

Throughout his *Meditations* (A.D. 167), the emperor and philosopher Marcus Aurelius, moving in the unstable world of Roman politics, continually reminded himself that any comment made about his character or achievements had to be subjected to the test of reason before he allowed it to affect his self-conception. "[One's decency] does not depend on the testimony of someone else," he insisted, thereby challenging his society's faith in an honour-based assessment of people. "Does what is praised become *better*? Does an emerald become *worse* if it isn't praised? And what of gold, ivory, a flower or a little plant?" Rather than be seduced by others' flattery or stung by their insults, Marcus aimed to take his bearings from the person he knew himself to be: "Will any man despise me? Let him see to it. But I will see to it that I may not be found doing or saying anything that deserves to be despised."

3.

We should not deduce from the foregoing that the condemnation or censure of others is invariably undeserved. Leaving the assessment of our worth to an intellectual conscience is not to be confused with expecting unconditional love. Unlike parents or lovers, who may value us whatever we do and however great our faults, philosophers do seek to apply criteria to their love—just not the shaky, unreasonable ones that the wider world is in danger of resorting to. There may indeed be times when an intellectual conscience will demand that we be harsher on ourselves than others are on us. Far from rejecting outright any hierarchy of success and failure, philosophy instead reconfigures the judging process, lending legitimacy to the idea that the mainstream value system may unfairly consign some people to disgrace and others to respectability. In the case of an injustice, it also helps us to hold on to the thought that we may be lovable even outside the halo of others' praise.

4.

Neither does philosophy deny the utility of certain kinds of anxiety. After all, as successful insomniacs have long suggested, it may be the anxious who survive best in the world.

Yet if we concede the worth of some feelings of anxiousness in helping us to find safety and develop our talents, we may be entitled to challenge the usefulness of *other* emotions in relation to precisely the same goals. We may feel envy, for instance, over a condition or possession that would in fact make us unhappy if we secured it. Likewise, we may experience ambitions unconnected to our real needs. Left to their own devices, our emotions are just as apt to push us towards indulgence, uncontrolled anger and self-destruction as they are towards health and virtue. Because it seems characteristic of these emotions to either undershoot or overshoot their targets, philosophers have counselled us to use our reasoning faculties to guide them to appropriate ends, asking ourselves whether what we want is really what we need and whether what we fear is truly what there is to fear.

In his *Eudemian Ethics* (circa 350 B.C.), Aristotle offered examples of the extremes towards which human behaviour will, when left unexamined, typically run. He also outlined an ideal, or golden mean, as stolid as it is wise, towards which we should aspire to direct that behaviour with the help of reason:

–	PHILOSOPHICAL IDEAL	+
Cowardice	Courage	Rashness
Stinginess	Liberality	Profligacy
Spinelessness	Gentleness	Rage
Boorishness	Wittiness	Buffoonery
Surliness	Friendliness	Obsequiousness

To these we might add:

Status lethargy	Ambition	Status hysteria

Intelligent Misanthropy

1.

If we have accepted well-founded criticism of our behaviour, paid heed to targeted anxieties about our ambitions and assumed proper responsibility for our failures, and yet if we continue to be accorded low status by our community, we may be tempted to adopt the approach taken by some of the greatest philosophers of the Western tradition: We may, through an unparanoid understanding of the warps of the value system around us, settle into a stance of intelligent misanthropy, free of both defensiveness and pride.

2.

When we begin to scrutinise the opinions of others, philosophers have long noted, we stand to make a discovery at once saddening and curiously liberating: we will discern that the views of the majority of the population on the majority of subjects are perforated with extraordinary confusion and error. Chamfort, voicing the misanthropic attitude of generations of philosophers both before and after him, put the matter simply: "Public opinion is the worst of all opinions."

The great defect, for Chamfort, consisted in the public's reluctance to submit its thinking to the rigours of rational examination, and its tendency to rely instead on intuition, emotion and custom. "One can be certain that every generally held idea, every received notion, will be an idiocy, because it has been able to appeal to a majority," the Frenchman observed, adding that what is flatteringly called common sense is usually little more than common *non*sense, suffering as it does from simplification and illogicality, prejudice and shallowness: "The most absurd customs and the most ridiculous ceremonies are everywhere excused by an appeal to the phrase, *but that's the tradition.* This is exactly what the Hottentots say when Europeans ask them why they eat grasshoppers and devour their body lice. *That's the tradition,* they explain."

3.

Painful though it may be to acknowledge the poverty of public opinion, the very act of doing so may somewhat ease our anxieties about status, mitigate our exhausting desire to ensure that others think well of us, and calm our panicked longing for signs of love.

The approval of others may be said to matter to us in two very different ways: materially, because the neglect of the community can bring with it physical discomfort and danger; and psychologically, because it can prove impossible to retain confidence in ourselves once others have ceased to accord us signs of respect.

It is in relation to this second consequence of inattention that the benefits of the philosophical approach best reveal themselves, for rather than allow every instance of opposition or neglect to wound us, we are invited by the philosophers first to examine the justice of others' behaviour. Only that which is both damning *and* true should be permitted to shatter our esteem. We should forever forswear the masochistic process wherein we seek another's approval before we have even asked ourselves whether that person's views deserve to be listened to—the process, that is, whereby we seek the love of those for whom, as we discover upon studying their minds, we have scant respect.

We might then start unrancorously to disdain certain others as much as they disdain us, planting our feet in a misanthropic stance for which the history of philosophy is replete with the most fortifying models.

4.

"We will gradually become indifferent to what goes on in the minds of other people when we acquire an adequate knowledge of the superficial and futile nature of their thoughts, of the narrowness of their views, of the paltriness of their sentiments, of the perversity of their opinions, and of the number of their errors . . . We shall then see that whoever attaches a lot of value to the opinions of others pays them too much honour," argued Arthur Schopenhauer, a leading model of philosophical misanthropy.

In *Parerga and Paralipomena* (1851), the philosopher proposed that nothing could more quickly correct the desire to be liked by others than a brief investigation into those others' true characters, which were, he asserted, for the most part excessively brutish and stupid. "In every country the principal entertainment of society has become card playing," he remarked with scorn. "It is a measure of the worth of society and the declared bankruptcy of all ideas and thoughts." The card players themselves, moreover, were usually sly and immoral: "The term *coquin méprisable* ['contemptible rogue'] is alas applicable to an unholy number of people in this world." And even worse, when people were *not* evil, they tended to be plain dull. Schopenhauer summed up the state of affairs by quoting Voltaire: "*La terre est couverte de gens qui ne méritent pas qu'on leur parle*" ("the earth swarms with people who are not worth talking to").

Ought we really to take the opinions of such people so seriously? asked Schopenhauer. Must we continue to let their verdicts govern what we make of ourselves? May our self-esteem sensibly be surrendered to a group of card players? And even if we manage somehow to win their respect, how much will it ever be worth? Or as Schopenhauer put the question, "Would a musician feel flattered by the loud applause of his audience if it were known to him that, with the exception of one or two, it consisted entirely of deaf people?"

5.

The disadvantage of this otherwise usefully clear-eyed view of humanity is that it may leave us with few friends. Schopenhauer's fellow philosophical misanthrope Chamfort admitted as much when he wrote: "Once we have resolved only to see those who will treat us morally and virtuously, reasonably and truthfully, without treating conventions, vanities and ceremonials as anything other than props of polite society; when we have taken this resolve (and we have to do so or we will end up foolish, weak or villainous), the result is that we will have to live more or less on our own."

Schopenhauer, for his part, accepted this possibility resignedly, affirming, "There is in the world only the choice between loneliness and vulgarity." All young people, he believed, should be taught "how to put up with loneliness . . . because the less a man is compelled to come into contact with others, the better off he is." Fortunately, after spending some time working and living in society, anyone with any sense must, suggested Schopenhauer, naturally feel "as little inclined to frequent association with others as schoolmasters to join the games of the boisterous and noisy crowds of children who surround them."

That said, deciding to avoid other people does not necessarily equate with having no desire whatsoever for company; it may simply reflect a dissatisfaction with what—or *who*—is available. Cynics are, in the end, only idealists with awkwardly high standards. In Chamfort's words, "It is sometimes said of a man who lives alone that he does not like society. This is like saying of a man that he does not like going for walks because he is not fond of walking at night in the forêt de Bondy."

6.

Dispensing advice from their isolated studies, philosophers have recommended that we follow the internal markers of our conscience rather than any external signs of approval or condemnation. What matters is not what we *seem* to be to a random group, but what we ourselves *know* we are. In Schopenhauer's words, "Every reproach can hurt only to the extent that it hits the mark. Whoever actually knows that he does not deserve a reproach can and will confidently treat it with contempt."

To heed the misanthropic philosophical counsel, we must surrender our puerile obsession with policing our own status—an impossible task in any case, and one that would in theory demand that we duel with, and either kill or be killed by, everyone who ever had a negative thought about us—and settle instead for the more solidly grounded satisfactions of a logically based sense of our worth.

II
ART

Introduction

1.

What is art good for? That question was in the air in Britain in the 1860s, and according to many commentators, the answer was, Not much. It was not art, after all, that had built the great industrial towns, laid the railways, dug the canals, expanded the empire and made Britain preeminent among nations. Indeed, art seemed capable of sapping the very qualities that had made such achievements possible, prolonged contact with it appeared to encourage effeminacy, introspection, homosexuality, gout and defeatism. In a speech in 1865, John Bright, member of Parliament for Birmingham, described cultured people as a pretentious cabal whose only claim to distinction was knowing "a smattering of the two dead languages of Greek and Latin." The Oxford academic Frederic Harrison (who might himself be presumed to boast some competency in the classics) took an equally caustic view of the benefits of prolonged communion with literature, history or painting. "Culture is a desirable quality in a critic of new books, and sits well on a possessor of *belles lettres*," he allowed, but "as applied to everyday life or politics, it means simply a turn for small fault-finding, love of selfish ease, and indecision in action. The man of culture is one of the poorest mortals alive. For simple pedantry and want of good sense no man is his equal. No assumption is too unreal, no end is too unpractical for him."

When these practical-minded disparagers cast their nets for a fitting exemplar of art's many deficiencies, they could find few more tempting potential trophies on the English literary scene than the poet and critic Matthew Arnold, professor of poetry at Oxford and the author of several slim volumes of melancholic verse that had been well received among a highbrow coterie. Not only was Arnold in the habit of walking the streets of London holding a silver-tipped cane, he also spoke in a quiet, high-pitched voice, sported peculiarly elongated sideburns, parted his hair in the middle and, worst of all, had the impudence to keep hinting, in a variety of newspaper articles and public lectures, that art might just be one of life's most important pursuits. This in an age when for the first time one could travel from London to Birmingham in a single morning, and Britain had earned itself the title of workshop of the world. The editors of the *Daily Telegraph*, stout upholder of industry and monarchy, were infuriated. They dubbed Arnold an "elegant Jeremiah" and "the high-priest of the kid-gloved persuasion," and mockingly accused him of trying to lure England's hardworking, sensible citizens "to leave their shops and duties behind them in order to recite songs, sing ballads and read essays."

2.

Arnold accepted the ribbing with good grace until finally, in 1869, he was goaded into composing and publishing a systematic, book-length defence of art, detailing what he believed it was for and what crucial functions it served, and must *continue* to serve, in life—even for a generation that had witnessed the invention of the foldaway umbrella and the steam engine.

Culture and Anarchy began by reviewing some of the charges that had been laid at art's door. In the eyes of many, Arnold acknowledged, it was nothing more than "a scented salve for human miseries, a religion breathing a spirit of cultivated inaction, making its believers refuse to lend a hand at uprooting evils. It is often summed up as being not practical or—as some critics more familiarly put it—all moonshine."

But far from being a mere salve, great art was in fact, Arnold argued, an effective antidote for life's deepest tensions and anxieties. However impractical it might seem to "the young lions of the *Daily Telegraph*," it was capable of presenting its audience with nothing less than an interpretation of and solution to the deficiencies of existence.

Every great work of art, suggested Arnold, was marked (directly or not) by the "desire to remove human error, clear human confusion, and diminish human misery," just as all great artists were imbued with the "aspiration to leave the world better and happier than they [found] it." They might not always realise this ambition through overtly political subject matter—indeed, might not even be aware of harbouring it at all—and yet embedded within their work, there was almost always some cry of protest against a status quo, and thus an impulse to correct the viewer's insight or teach him to perceive beauty, to help him understand pain or to reanimate his sensitivities, to nurture his capacity for empathy or rebalance his moral perspective through sadness or laughter. Arnold concluded his argument with the idea upon which this chapter is built: Art, he insisted, was "the criticism of life."

3.

What are we to understand by Arnold's phrase? First, and perhaps most obvious, that life is a phenomenon in need of criticism, for we are, as fallen creatures, in permanent danger of worshipping false gods, of failing to understand ourselves and misinterpreting the behaviour of others, of growing unproductively anxious or desirous, and of losing ourselves to vanity and error. Surreptitiously and beguilingly, then, with humour or gravity, works of art—novels, poems, plays, paintings or films—can function as vehicles to explain our condition to us. They may act as guides to a truer, more judicious, more intelligent understanding of the world.

Given that few things are more in need of criticism (or of insight and analysis) than our approach to status and its distribution, it is hardly surprising that so many artists across time should have created works that in some way contest the methods by which people are accorded rank in society. The history of art is filled with challenges—ironic, angry, lyrical, sad or amusing—to the status system.

Art and Snobbery

1.

Jane Austen began writing *Mansfield Park* in the spring of 1811 and published it three years later. The novel tells the story of Fanny Price, a shy, modest young girl from a penniless family in Portsmouth, who, in order to relieve her parents of some of their burden, agrees to go and live with her aunt and uncle, the plutocratic Sir Thomas and Lady Bertram, at Mansfield Park, their stately home. Standing at the pinnacle of the English county hierarchy, the Bertrams are spoken of with awe and reverence by their neighbours. Their two daughters, Maria and Julia, are coquettish teenagers who enjoy a generous clothes allowance and have their own horses; their eldest son, Tom, is a bumptious and casually insensitive lout who spends most of his time in London clubs, lubricating his friendships with champagne while focusing his hopes for the future on his father's death and the inheritance of the paternal estate and title. Adept though they are at affecting the self-deprecating manner so beloved of the English upper classes, Sir Thomas Bertram and his family never forget (nor allow others to forget) their superior rank or all the distinction that must naturally accompany their ownership of a large, landscaped garden through which deer wander in the quiet hours between tea and dinner.

Fanny may live under the same roof as the Bertrams, but she cannot be on an equal footing with them. Her privileges have been given to her at the discretion of Sir Thomas; her cousins patronise her; the neighbours regard her with a mixture of suspicion and pity; and she is treated by most of the family like a lady-in-waiting whose company they may take some modest pleasure in but whose feelings they are fortunately never under any prolonged obligation to consider.

Before Fanny's arrival at Mansfield Park, Austen allows us to eavesdrop on the family's anxieties about their new charge. "I hope she will not tease my poor pug," remarks Lady Bertram. The children wonder what Fanny's clothes will look like and whether she will speak French and know the names of the kings and queens of England. Sir Thomas Bertram, despite having proffered the invitation to Fanny's parents in the first place, expects the worst: "We shall probably see much to wish altered in her and should prepare ourselves for gross ignorance, some meanness of opinions and a very distressing vulgarity of manner." His sister-in-law Mrs. Norris insists that Fanny must be told early on that she is not, and never will be, *one of them.* Sir Thomas avers, "We must make her remember that she is not a *Miss Bertram.* I should wish to see Fanny and her cousins very good friends but they cannot be equals. Their rank, fortune, rights and expectations will always be different."

Fanny's advent seems only to confirm the family's prejudices against those who have failed to grow up on estates with landscaped gardens. Julia and Maria discover that Fanny owns just one nice dress, speaks no French and doesn't know anything. "Only think, my cousin cannot put the map of Europe together," Julia exclaims to her aunt and mother, "nor can she tell the principal rivers in Russia and she has never heard of Asia Minor—How strange! Did you ever hear anything so stupid? Do you know, we asked her last night, which way she would go to get to Ireland and she said, she should cross to the Isle of Wight." "Yes, my dear," replies Mrs. Norris, "but you and your sister are blessed with wonderful memories, and your poor cousin has probably none at all. You must make allowances for her and pity her deficiency."

The novel's author takes a little longer than Mrs. Norris to make up her mind as to who is deficient, and in what capacity. For a decade or more, Austen follows Fanny patiently down the corridors and into the reception rooms of Mansfield Park; listens to her mutterings in her bedroom and on her walks around the gardens; reads her letters; eavesdrops on her observations about her adoptive family; watches the movements of her eyes and mouth; and peers into her soul. In the process, she picks up on a rare, quiet virtue of her heroine's.

Unlike Julia and Maria, Fanny does not concern herself with whether every young man she meets has a large house and a title. She is offended by her cousin Tom's indifferent cruelty and arrogance and flinches from her aunt's financial considerations of her neighbours. The Bertrams themselves, meanwhile, so highly ranked within the conventional county status hierarchy, are more troublingly placed in that *other,* even more exacting status system, the novelist's hierarchy of preference. Maria and her suitor, Mr. Rushworth, may have horses, houses and inheritances, but Jane Austen sees how they go about falling in love, and she cannot forgive them for it:

"Mr. Rushworth was from the first struck with the beauty of Miss Bertram, and being inclined to marry, soon fancied himself in love. Being now in her twenty-first year, Maria Bertram was beginning to think matrimony a duty; and as a marriage with Mr. Rushworth would give her the enjoyment of a larger income than her father's, as well as ensure her a house in town, it became her evident duty to marry Mr. Rushworth if she could."

Who's Who or *Debrett's Guide to the Top Families of England* might have held Maria and Mr. Rushworth in high esteem. After such a paragraph, Austen cannot—nor will she let her readers. The novelist exchanges the standard lens through which people are viewed in society, a lens that magnifies wealth and power, for a moral lens whose focal point is subtler qualities of character. Seen through this lens, the high and mighty may become small, and forgotten and retiring figures loom large. Within the world of the novel, virtue is shown to be distributed without regard to material wealth. The rich and well-mannered are not ipso facto good, nor the poor and unschooled necessarily bad. Goodness may be inherent in the lame, ugly child, the destitute porter, the hunchback in the attic or the girl ignorant of the most basic facts of geography. Certainly Fanny possesses no elegant dresses, has no money and can't speak French, but by the end of *Mansfield Park,* she has been revealed as the one member of her extended family endowed with a noble soul, while all the others, despite their titles and accomplishments, have fallen into moral confusion. Sir Thomas Bertram has allowed snobbery to ruin the education of his children, his daughters have married for money and paid an emotional price for that decision, and his wife has let her heart turn to stone. The hierarchical system of Mansfield Park has been turned on its head.

Austen does not, of course, make explicit her concept of true hierarchy, boxing our ears with a preacher's bluntness; she instead enlists our sympathies and marshals our abhorrence for its opposite with the skill and humour of a great novelist. She does not *tell* us why her moral priorities are important; she *shows* us why within the context of a story that also manages to make us laugh and that takes such a strong hold on our imagination that we want to finish supper early so we may read on. As we reach the end of *Mansfield Park,* we are invited to go back into our own world—the world from which Austen has drawn us aside—and respond to its inhabitants as she has taught us to do, detecting and recoiling from greed, arrogance and pride and seeking out the good in ourselves and in others.

Austen once modestly and famously described her art as "the little bit (two inches wide) of ivory on which I work with so fine a brush, as produces little effect after much labour," but her novels are suffused with greater ambitions. Each one attempts, by examining what she called "three or four families in a country village," to criticise and so alter our lives.

2.

Austen was not alone in her aspirations. Almost every great novel of the nineteenth and twentieth centuries stages an assault on, or at the very least harbours scepticism regarding, the accepted social hierarchy, and each offers some sort of redefinition of precedence according to moral worth rather than financial assets or bloodlines. Only on rare occasions are the heroes and heroines of fiction the type of people to whom *Debrett's* or *Who's Who* would give priority. In the pages of these works, the first become something like the last, and the last something like the first. For example, in Balzac's *Le Père Goriot* (1834), it is not Madame de Nucingen, with her gilded house, who solicits our sympathies, but the toothless old Goriot, eking out his days in a putrid boardinghouse. Similarly, in Hardy's *Jude the Obscure* (1895), it is not the Oxford dons whom we respect, but the impoverished, ill-schooled stonemason who repairs the gargoyles of the university's colleges.

Standing witness to hidden lives, novels may act as conceptual counterweights to dominant hierarchical realities. They can reveal that the maid now busying herself with lunch is a creature of rare sensitivity and moral greatness, while the baron who laughs raucously and owns a silver mine has a heart both withered and acrid.

If we are inclined to forget the lesson, it may be in part because what is best in other people seldom has a chance to express itself in the sort of external achievements that attract and hold our ordinary, vagabond attention. George Eliot's *Middlemarch* (1872) begins with a discussion of this human tendency to admire only the most obvious exploits, as the author draws an unlikely comparison between her heroine and Saint Theresa of Avila (1512–82). Thanks to good luck and circumstance, because she came from a wealthy and well-connected family, Saint Theresa was able (Eliot reminds us) to embody her goodness and creativity in concrete acts. She founded seventeen convents; communicated with some of the most devout individuals of her day; wrote an autobiography and a number of treatises on prayer and vision; and became not only one of the principal saints of the Roman Catholic Church but perhaps its greatest mystic. By the time of her death, Theresa could claim a status equal to her virtue. In that, she was singularly blessed, Eliot suggests, citing the legions of people in the world who, though no less intelligent or creative than the Spanish saint, nonetheless fail ever to externalise their finer qualities in useful actions. Through a combination of their own errors and unhelpful social conditions, these less fortunate mortals are thereby condemned to a status that bears scant relation to their inner worth. According to the novelist, "Many Theresas have been born who found for themselves no epic life; only a life of mistakes, the offspring of a certain spiritual grandeur ill-matched with a meanness of opportunity." It is the life of one such woman, Dorothea Brooke, living in an English town in the first half of the nineteenth century, that *Middlemarch* sets out to recount, the novel as a whole offering a critique of the world's habit of neglecting what Eliot calls "spiritual grandeur" whenever it is unlinked to "long-recognised deeds."

Dorothea may well possess many of the same virtues as Saint Theresa, but they are not apparent to a world attentive only to the symbols of status. Because she first marries a sickly clergyman and then, little more than a year after his death, gives up her estate to wed her late husband's cousin (who has no property and is not well-born), society insists that she cannot be a "good woman," and everyone in the village gossips about her and shuns her company. "Certainly those determining acts of her life were not ideally beautiful," Eliot herself concedes. "They were the mixed result of a young and noble impulse struggling amidst the conditions of an imperfect social state." But then, in some of the most quietly stirring lines in all of nineteenth-century English fiction, Eliot asks us to look beyond

Status in Life vs. Status in Novels

NOVEL	HIGH STATUS IN NOVEL, LOW STATUS IN LIFE	HIGH STATUS IN LIFE, LOW STATUS IN NOVEL
Joseph Andrews (1742) Henry Fielding	Joseph Andrews Parson Adams	Lady Booby Parson Trulliber
Vanity Fair (1848) William Thackeray	William Dobbin Amelia Sedley	Becky Sharp Jos Sedley George Osborne Sir Pitt Crawley Rawdon Crawley
Bleak House (1853) Charles Dickens	Esther Summerson Jo Bucket	The Dedlocks Mr. Chadband Mrs. Jellyby Richard Carstone
The Woman in White (1860) Wilkie Collins	Anne Catherick Marian Halcombe	Sir Percival Glyde Count Fosco Frederick Fairlie
The Way We Live Now (1875) Anthony Trollope	Paul Montague Mr. Brehgert John Crumb	Augustus Melmotte Marie Melmotte Sir Felix Carbury Dolly Longestaffe Georgiana Longestaffe Lord Nidderdale

Dorothea's socially unacceptable marriages and her lack of achievements in order to recognise that, in its domestic and circumscribed way, her character is indeed no less saintly than Theresa's must have been: "Her finely-touched spirit had its fine issues, even though they were not widely visible. Her full nature spent itself in channels which had no great name on the earth. But the effect of her being on those around her was incalculably diffusive: for the growing good of the world is partly dependent on unhistoric acts; and that things are not so ill with you and me as they might have been, is half owing to the number who lived faithfully a hidden life and rest in unvisited tombs."

Lines that may be stretched to define a whole conception of the novel: an artistic medium to help us understand and appreciate the value of every hidden life that rests in an unvisited tomb. "If art does not enlarge men's sympathies, it does nothing morally," knew George Eliot.

In Zadie Smith's *White Teeth* (2000), we meet Samad, a middle-aged Bangladeshi employed as a waiter in an Indian restaurant in London. He is treated roughly by his superiors, works until three in the morning and has to wait upon coarse customers who magnanimously reward him with fifteen-pence tips. Samad dreams of somehow recovering his dignity, of escaping the material and psychological consequences of his status. He longs to alert others to the riches that lie buried within him, unsuspected by patrons who barely look up when he takes their orders ("Go Bye Ello Sag, please" and "Chicken Jail Fret See wiv Chips, fanks"). He imagines wearing a sign around his neck, a white placard that would read, in letters large enough for the whole world to see:

I AM NOT A WAITER. I HAVE BEEN A STUDENT, A SCIENTIST, A SOLDIER, MY WIFE IS CALLED ALSANA, WE LIVE IN EAST LONDON BUT WE WOULD LIKE TO MOVE NORTH. I AM A MUSLIM BUT ALLAH HAS FORSAKEN ME OR I HAVE FORSAKEN ALLAH, I'M NOT SURE. I HAVE A FRIEND— ARCHIE—AND OTHERS. I AM FORTY-NINE BUT WOMEN STILL TURN IN THE STREET. SOMETIMES.

He never does acquire such a placard, but he gets the next best thing: a novelist who supplies him with a voice. The entire novel in which Samad appears is in a sense a giant placard that will help to make it just that much harder for its readers ever again to order Chicken Jail Fret See in such a casually indifferent, casually dehumanizing manner.

The best novels expand and extend our sympathies. Taken together, they may in fact stand as one long procession of signs that tell the world:

I AM NOT JUST A WAITER, A DIVORCEE, AN ADULTERER, A THIEF, AN UNEDUCATED MAN, A PECULIAR CHILD, A MURDERER, A CONVICT, A FAILURE AT SCHOOL OR A SHY PERSON WITH NOTHING TO SAY FOR HERSELF.

3.

Paintings, too, can challenge society's normal understanding of who or what matters.

Jean-Baptiste Chardin painted his *Meal for a Convalescent* in circa 1738. A modestly dressed woman stands in a sparsely furnished room, peeling an egg for a sick person we cannot see. It is an ordinary moment in the life of an ordinary person. Why paint such a thing? For much of Chardin's career, critics persisted in asking that question. It irked them that this gifted artist devoted all his attention to loaves of bread, broken plates, knives and forks, apples and pears and working- or lower-middle-class characters going about their business in humble kitchens and living rooms.

These were certainly not the sorts of subjects that a great artist was supposed to paint, according to the canons laid down by the French

Jean-Baptiste Chardin, Meal for a Convalescent, *c. 1738*

Academy of Fine Arts. Upon the academy's founding by Louis XIV, in 1648, its officers had ranked the different pictorial genres in a hierarchy of importance. At the very top was history painting, with its canvases expressing the nobility of ancient Greece and Rome or illustrating biblical morality tales. Second came portraiture, especially of kings and queens. Third was landscape, distantly followed by what was dismissively described as "genre painting," depicting scenes from the domestic lives of commoners. This artistic hierarchy corresponded directly with the social hierarchy of the world beyond the artists' studios, where a king sitting on a horse and surveying his estates was deemed naturally superior to a plainly dressed woman peeling an egg.

But within Chardin's art lies an implicit subversion of any vision of life that could dismiss as valueless a woman's domestic labours or even a piece of old pottery catching the afternoon sun ("Chardin has taught us that a pear can be as full of life as a woman, that a jug is as beautiful as a precious stone," observed Marcel Proust).

The history of painting provides Chardin with a tiny coterie of fellow spirits, and us with a handful of great correctives to our customary notions of importance. One of the more notable, for our purposes, was the Welsh painter Thomas Jones, who worked in Italy, first in Rome and then in Naples, between 1776 and 1783. It was in Naples, in early April 1782, that Jones completed what may be two of the finest oils on paper in the whole of Western art, *Rooftops, Naples* (which hangs in the Ashmolean Museum in Oxford) and *Buildings in Naples* (in the National Museum of Wales, Cardiff).

The views captured by Jones remain a familiar feature of many Mediterranean cities and towns, where houses are pressed together along narrow streets and give out onto the naked flanks of neighbouring buildings. On a warm afternoon, the streets tend to be quiet and the windows half shuttered. One may glimpse the outline of a woman moving inside a sitting room or the dark mass of a man

asleep on a bed. Occasionally one may hear the cry of a child or the rustle made by an old woman as she hangs laundry on a terrace with a rusting handrail.

Jones shows us how the intense southern light falls on walls of chipped and weathered stucco, bringing out every indentation and fracture, the painted surface evoking the passage of time as effectively as the rough, worn hands of a fisherman. Soon April will give way to May, and then the blank, dead heat of summer to furious winter storms, which themselves, after an apparent eternity, will once again cede their place to tentative spring sunshine. Jones's stone and stucco are close kin to clay and plaster and to the fragments of pitted rock that stud so many Mediterranean hillsides. The confu-

Thomas Jones, Rooftops, Naples, *1782*

sion of buildings in these works affords us an impression of a town in which a multiplicity of lives is unfolding in every window—lives no less complicated than those portrayed in the great novels, lives of passion and boredom, playfulness and despair.

How seldom do we notice rooftops; how easily are our eyes drawn instead to the more flamboyant attractions of a Roman temple or Renaissance church. But Jones has held up the ignored scene for our contemplation and rendered its latent beauty visible, so that never again will southern rooftops count for nothing in our understanding of happiness.

The nineteenth-century Dane Christen Købke was another who strove, through his painting, to subvert conventional notions of

Thomas Jones, Buildings in Naples, *1782*

what should be considered valuable. Between 1832 and 1838, he tire-
lessly explored the suburbs, streets and gardens of his native Copen-
hagen. He painted a couple of cows ruminating in a field on a
summer afternoon, and caught two men and their wives disembark-
ing from a small sailing boat on the shore of a lake. (It is evening, but
darkness seems in no hurry to settle over the land; an echo of day-
light hovers for an apparent eternity in the vast sky, presaging a gentle night on which windows may be left open, and a lucky few will
sleep outside on blankets spread across the grass.) He reproduced
the view from the roof of Frederiksborg Castle, looking out onto a
neat patchwork of fields, gardens and farms, an image of an ordered
community content to enjoy the snatched pleasures of daily life.

Christen Købke, View from the Embankment of Lake Sortedam, *1838*

Christen Købke, The Roof of Frederiksborg Castle, *1834–1835*

Collectively, these works by Købke, Jones and Chardin appear to suggest that if such commonplaces as the sky on a summer's evening, a pitted wall heated by the sun and the face of an unknown woman as she peels an egg for a sick person are truly among the loveliest sights we may hope ever to lay our eyes on, then perhaps we are honour-bound to question the value of much that we have been taught to respect and aspire to.

It may seem far-fetched to hang a quasipolitical programme on a jug placed on a sideboard, or on a cow grazing in a pasture, but the moral of a work by one of these three painters may reach dauntingly far beyond the limited meaning we are generally prepared to attribute to a piece of painted cloth or paper. Like Jane Austen and George Eliot, the great artists of everyday life may help us to correct many of our snobbish preconceptions regarding what there is to esteem and honour in the world.

Christen Købke, A View in the Neighbourhood of the Lime Kiln, *1834–1835*

Tragedy

1.

Our fear of failing at various tasks would likely be much less were it not for our awareness of how harshly failure tends to be viewed and interpreted by others. Fear of the material consequences of failure is thus compounded by fear of the unsympathetic attitude of the world towards those who have failed, exemplified by its haunting proclivity to refer to them as "losers"—a word callously signifying both that they have lost and that they have, at the same time, forfeited any right to sympathy for losing.

So unforgiving is the tone in which the majority of ruined lives are discussed, indeed, that if the protagonists of many works of art—among them Oedipus, Antigone, Lear, Othello, Emma Bovary, Anna Karenina, Hedda Gabler and Tess—had had their fates chewed over by a cabal of colleagues or old school acquaintances, they almost certainly would not have emerged well from the process. They might have fared even worse if the press had got hold of them:

Othello:	Love-Crazed Immigrant Kills Senator's Daughter
Oedipus the King:	Royal in Incest Shocker
Madame Bovary:	Shopaholic Adulteress Swallows Arsenic after Credit Fraud

If something about these headlines seems incongruous, it may be because we are used to thinking of the subjects to which they refer as being inherently complex and naturally deserving of a solemn and respectful attitude, rather than the prurient and damning one that newspapers all but automatically take vis-à-vis their victims. But in truth, nothing about these figures makes them inevitable objects of concern or respect. That the legendary failed characters of art seem so noble to us has little to do with their individual qualities per se and almost everything to do with how we have been taught to consider them by their creators and chroniclers.

There is one art form in particular that has, since its inception, dedicated itself to recounting stories of great failure without recourse to mockery or judgement. While not absolving its subjects of responsibility for their actions, it has nonetheless succeeded in offering and eliciting for those involved in catastrophes—disgraced statesmen, murderers, the bankrupt, emotional compulsives—a level of sympathy owed, but rarely extended, to every human.

2.

At its inception, in the theatres of ancient Greece in the sixth century B.C., tragic drama followed a hero—usually someone highborn, a king or a famous warrior—from prosperity and acclaim to ruin and shame, a downfall always brought on by some error of his own. The telling of the story—the *way* it was told—was intended to leave audiences at once hesitant to condemn the protagonist for what had befallen him and humbled by the realisation of how easily *they* might be ruined if ever they found themselves in a similar situation.

If the newspaper, with its lexicon of perverts and weirdos, failures and losers, lies at one end of the spectrum of understanding, then tragedy lies at the other. In its ambition to build bridges between the guilty and the apparently blameless, in its challenging of ordinary conceptions of responsibility, it stands as the most psychologically sophisticated, most respectful account of how a human being may be dishonoured without at the same time losing his or her right to be heard.

3.

In his *Poetics* (circa 350 B.C.), Aristotle attempted to define the core constituents of an effective tragedy. There needed to be one central character, he postulated; the action had to unfold in a relatively compressed length of time; and, unsurprisingly, "the change in the hero's fortunes" must be "not from misery to happiness" but, on the contrary, "from happiness to misery."

There were two additional, more telling requirements. A tragic hero had to be someone who was neither especially good nor especially bad, an everyday, regular kind of human being at the ethical level, someone to whom the audience could easily relate, whose character combined a range of good qualities with one or more common defects—for example, excessive pride or anger or impulsiveness. And finally, this figure must make a spectacular mistake, not out of any profoundly evil motive, but rather due to what Aristotle termed in Greek a *hamartia* (an "error in judgement"), a temporary lapse, or a factual or emotional slip. And from this would flow the most terrible *peripeteia*, or "reversal of fortune," over the course of which the hero would lose everything he held dear before at last almost certainly paying for his blunder with his life.

Pity for the hero, and fear for oneself based on an identification with him, would be the natural emotional outcome of following such a tale. The tragic work would educate us to acquire modesty about our capacity to avoid disaster and at the same time guide us to feel sympathy for those who had met with it. We were to leave the theatre disinclined ever again to adopt an easy, superior tone towards the fallen and the failed.

Aristotle's great insight was that the degree of sympathy we will feel regarding another's fiasco is directly proportional to how easy or difficult it is for us to imagine ourselves, under like circumstances, making a similar mistake. How could sane, normal people *do* such things, we may wonder upon hearing of real-life lapsers who have married rashly, slept with a member of their own family, murdered their lover in a jealous frenzy, lied to their employer, stolen money or allowed an avaricious streak to ruin their career. Confident that cast-iron walls separate our nature and situation from theirs, comfortable in the well-broken-in saddle of our high horse, we have exchanged our capacity to be tolerant for detachment and derision.

It is the tragedian's task, then, to force us to confront an almost unbearable truth: every folly or myopia of which any human being in history has been guilty may be traced back to some aspect of our collective nature. Because we each bear within ourselves the whole of the human condition, in its worst and best aspects, any one of us might be capable of doing anything at all, or nothing, under the right—or rather the most horribly wrong—conditions. Once theatregoers have experienced this truism, they may willingly dismount from their high horses and feel their powers of sympathy and humility return, enhanced. They may accept how readily their own lives might be shattered if certain of their more regrettable character traits, which have until now invited no serious trouble, were one day to coincide with a situation that allowed them unlimited and catastrophic dominion, leaving these heretofore innocents no less shamed and wretched than the unfortunate soul suffering beneath the headline "Royal in Incest Shocker."

4.

The play that most perfectly accorded with Aristotle's conception of the tragic art form was Sophocles' *Oedipus the King*, first performed in Athens at the Festival of Dionysus in the spring of 430 B.C.

Sophocles' Oedipus, the king of Thebes, is worshipped by his people for his benevolent rule and for the wisdom he displayed many years before in outwitting the Sphinx and driving it from the city—which exploit earned him his throne. For all his good qualities, however, the king is not flawless: most notably, he is impetuous and prone to rage. Long ago, in fact, during one particularly violent outburst on the road to Thebes, he killed an obstinate old man who refused to get out of his way. That incident was largely obscured, though, by subsequent events, as Oedipus's victory over the Sphinx was followed by a period of prosperity and security for the city. During this time, Oedipus also married the beautiful Jocasta, widow of his predecessor, King Laius, who had died under unexplained circumstances while fighting with a young man just outside Thebes.

As the play opens, a new disaster no less menacing than the Sphinx has descended upon the city: a peculiar plague for which no cure can be found is ravaging the population. Desperate, the people turn to the royal family for help. Oedipus's brother-in-law, Creon, is dispatched to seek answers from the oracle of Apollo at Delphi, who gnomically explains that Thebes is being forced to pay the price for an unclean thing within its walls. Creon and others at court decide this must be an allusion to the unsolved murder of the previous monarch. Oedipus agrees and vows that he personally will see to it that the killer is found and mercilessly punished.

Jocasta's face darkens as she hears all this. As if for the first time, she remembers another prophecy from long ago, when King Laius was warned that he would perish by his son's hand. To avert that outcome, Laius had ordered that the baby boy Jocasta later bore him be taken to a mountainside and left there to die.

But of course, there was no getting around fate: the shepherd charged with the task took pity on the infant and instead, in secret, gave him to the king of Corinth to raise as his own. When this boy reached maturity, yet another oracle revealed to the Corinthian king and queen that he would someday kill his father and marry his mother. Determined to avoid such crimes, Oedipus left his adoptive home and travelled the length of Greece, ending up . . . on the road leading into Thebes.

Jocasta, the first to comprehend what has happened, retires to her rooms in the royal palace and hangs herself. Oedipus finds her swinging from the rafters, cuts down her body and pierces his own eyes with the brooch from her dress. He embraces his two daughters, Ismene and Antigone, who are yet too young to understand the nightmare that is their parents' situation, and then sends himself into exile, to wander the earth in shame until his death.

5.

We might, here, offer the rejoinder that patricide and incest are judgement errors of a sort that not many of us are liable to make. But the extraordinary dimensions of Oedipus's *hamartia* do not detract from the more universal features of the play. Rather, the story moves us insofar as it reflects shocking aspects of everyman's character and condition: the way apparently small missteps can result in the gravest of consequences; the blindness we often suffer with regard to the effects of our actions; our fatuous tendency to presume that we are in conscious command of our destiny; the speed and finality with which everything we cherish may be lost to us; and the mysterious and unvanquishable forces—for Sophocles, "fate"—against which our weak powers of reason and foresight are pitted. Oedipus is by no means without fault: he hubristically believes himself to have escaped the oracles' prophecies and lazily accedes to his subjects' high opinion of him. His pride and hot temper cause him to pick a fight with King Laius, and his emotional cowardice thereafter prevents him from linking the murder to the earlier prophecies. And his self-righteousness permits him to ignore the crime for many years and then to chide Creon for hinting at his guilt.

Yet even if Oedipus bears responsibility for his own fate, the tragic art form renders any easy condemnation impossible. It apportions blame to him without denying him sympathy. As Aristotle imagined, the audience must leave the theatre appalled yet compassionate, haunted by the universal implications of the concluding message of the chorus:

People of Thebes, my countrymen, look on Oedipus.
He solved the famous riddle with his brilliance,
He rose to power, a man beyond all power.
Who could behold his greatness without envy?
Now what a black sea of terror has overwhelmed him.
Now as we keep our watch and wait the final day,
Count no man happy till he dies, free of pain at last.

6.

If a tragic work allows us to feel a much greater degree of sympathy for others' failings than we ordinarily might, it is principally because the form itself seeks to plumb the origins of failure. To know more is, in this context, necessarily to understand and forgive more. Tragedy leads us artfully through the minuscule, often innocent acts that connect heroes' and heroines' prosperity to their downfall, disclosing along the way the perverse relationships between intentions and consequences. Thus well informed, we are unlikely to maintain for long the indifferent or vengeful tone we might have clung to had we merely read the bare bones of the very same stories of failure in the popular press.

In the summer of 1848, a terse item appeared in many newspapers across Normandy. A twenty-seven-year-old woman named Delphine Delamare, née Couturier, of Ry, a small town not far from Rouen, had tired of the routines of marriage and, after running up huge debts on extravagant purchases of clothing and household goods, had embarked on an affair. Under emotional and financial pressure, she had at last taken her own life by swallowing arsenic.

Madame Delamare had left behind a young daughter and a distraught husband, Eugène, who had once studied medicine in Rouen. In his post as a health officer in Ry, the papers noted, Delamare was loved by his patients and respected by the community.

Among those who saw this item was a twenty-seven-year-old aspiring novelist named Gustave Flaubert. The story of Madame Delamare would stay with him, becoming something of an obsession (it even followed him on a journey around Egypt and Palestine) until, in September 1851, he settled down to work on it. *Madame Bovary* would be published in Paris six years later.

One of the many things that happened when Madame Delamare, the adulteress from Ry, turned into Madame Bovary, the adulteress from Yonville, was that her life began to expand beyond the dimensions of a black-and-white morality tale. As a newspaper story, the case of Delphine Delamare had been seized upon by conservative provincial commentators as an example of the declining respect for marriage among the young, of the increasing commercialisation of society and of the loss of religious values. But for Flaubert, art was the very antithesis of crass moralism. It was a realm in which human motives and behaviour could for once be explored in real depth, with a sensitivity that would make a mockery of any desire on the part of the reader to construe saints or sinners. Flaubert's audience would hear of Emma's naive ideas about love, but they would also learn where these had come from: they would follow her back to her childhood, read over her shoulder at the convent, sit with her and her father through long summer afternoons in their kitchen in Tostes, as the squeals and clucks of pigs and chickens drifted in from the yard. They would watch as she and Charles stumbled into an ill-matched marriage, and then witness Charles's seduction by his own loneliness and a young woman's physical charms. They would feel Emma's need to escape her cloistered life, ironically fuelled by her lack of experience with men outside third-rate romantic literature. Readers would be able to—would *have* to—sympathise equally with Charles's complaints about Emma and with Emma's about Charles. Flaubert seemed to take an almost deliberate pleasure in everywhere unsettling his readers' inclination to find comfortable answers: no sooner had he presented Emma in a positive light, for example, than he would undercut her with a mordant remark. And then, just as readers were losing patience with her, just as they began to think her nothing more than a selfish hedonist, he would draw them back to her, tell them something about her inner life that would make them cry. By the time she lost her status in her community, crammed arsenic into her mouth and lay down in her bedroom to await her death, few who knew her history would be disposed to judge her.

We set down Flaubert's novel feeling a mixture of fear and sadness—at how we are all made to live before we can even begin to know how, at how limited is our understanding of ourselves and others, at how great and catastrophic are the consequences of our actions, and how often pitiless and uncompromising the responses of upstanding members of the community when we err.

7.

As members of the audience of any tragic work, whether dramatic or literary, we are as far as it is possible to get from the spirit of the headline Shopaholic Adulteress Swallows Arsenic, insofar as the genre of tragedy itself will have inspired us to abandon ordinary life's simplified perspective on failure and defeat, and rendered us infinitely more generous towards the foolishness and transgressions endemic to human nature.

A world in which a majority had imbibed the lessons implicit within tragic art would be one in which the consequences of our failures would necessarily cease to weigh upon us so heavily.

Comedy

1.

The summer of 1831 found King Louis-Philippe of France in a confident mood. The political and economic chaos of the July Revolution, which had brought him to power the year before, was gradually giving way to prosperity and order. He had in place a competent team of officials led by his prime minister, Casimir Périer, and on tours around the northern and eastern parts of his realm had been given a hero's welcome by the provincial middle classes. He lived in splendour in the Palais-Royal in Paris; attended weekly banquets in his honour; loved eating (especially foie gras and game) and had a vast personal fortune and a loving wife and children.

But there was one cloud on Louis-Philippe's otherwise sunny

Ary Scheffer, King Louis-Philippe of France, *1835*

horizon: in late 1830, an unknown twenty-eight-year-old artist by the name of Charles Philipon had launched a satirical magazine, *La Caricature*, in which he now graphically transformed the head of the king (whom he also accused of corruption and incompetence on a grand scale) into a pear. Unflattering as Philipon's cartoons were, depicting Louis-Philippe with swollen cheeks and a bulbous forehead, they carried an additional, implied disparagement: the French word *poire*, meaning not only "pear" but "fathead" or "mug," neatly conveyed a less-than-respectful sentiment regarding the monarch's administrative abilities.

Enraged by the dig, Louis-Philippe instructed his agents to stop production of the magazine and to buy up all unsold copies from Parisian kiosks. When these measures failed to deter Philipon, prosecutors in November 1831 charged him with having "caused offence to the person of the king," and summoned him to appear in court. Speaking before a packed chamber, the caricaturist sardonically thanked the government for arresting such a dangerous man as himself, but then he suggested that the prosecutors had been negligent in their pursuit of the king's detractors. They should make it their priority, he insisted, to go after anything in the shape of a pear; indeed, even pears themselves should be locked up. There were thousands of them on trees all over France, and every one a criminal fit for incarceration. The court was not amused. Philipon was sentenced to six months in prison, and when he dared to repeat the pear joke in a new magazine, *Le Charivari*, the following year, he was sent straight back to jail. In all, he spent two years behind bars for drawing the monarch as a piece of fruit.

Three decades earlier, Napoleon Bonaparte, then the most powerful man in Europe, had himself felt no less vulnerable to the prick of satire. On coming to power in 1799, he had ordered the closure of every satirical paper in Paris and told his police chief, Joseph Fouché, that he would not tolerate cartoonists' taking liberties with his appearance. He preferred to leave his visual representation to Jacques-Louis David. He commissioned the great painter to depict him leading his armies across the Alps, looking heroic on a horse, and so pleased was he with the result—*Napoleon Crossing the Saint-Bernard* (1801)—that he turned to David again to record the apogee of his triumphs, his coronation in Notre-Dame in December 1804. It was an occasion of high pomp: all the grandees of France were gathered, Pope Pius VII officiated and delegations had been dispatched by most European countries to pay their respects. Jean-François Lesueur had composed a suitably imposing score. Blessing Napoleon, the pope called out across the hushed cathedral, "*Vivat imperator in aeternam.*"

Upon completing his rendition of the scene, *Le Sacre de Joséphine*, in November 1807, David offered it "to my illustrious master." A jubilant Napoleon made the painter an officer of the Legion of Honour in recognition of his "services to art" and proclaimed to him, as he pinned the medal on his chest, "You have brought good taste back to France."

Not all artists, however, saw Napoleon as David did. A couple of years before the unveiling of *Le Sacre de Joséphine*, the English caricaturist James Gillray had published a very different view of the event, which he entitled *The Grand Coronation Procession of Napoleone the 1st Emperor of France* (1805). But there was never any talk of awarding *him* the Legion of Honour for restoring good taste to France.

Jacques-Louis David, Le Sacre de Joséphine, *1807*

Gillray's drawing shows a preening, swollen, strutting emperor at the head of a parade of flunkies, flatterers and prisoners. Pope Pius VII is pictured, but he is hardly the holy man of David's version: here, the papal robes shelter a choirboy, who lets slip his mask to reveal the face of the devil. Josephine, far from the fresh-faced damsel David would paint, is an acne-scarred balloon. Carrying the train of the emperor are representatives from the countries already conquered by Napoleon—Prussia, Spain and Holland—whose participation does not appear to be precisely voluntary. Behind them are rows of shackled French soldiers, their condition indicating that this is not an emperor to whom the people have given power willingly. Keeping these last in line is Police Chief Fouché, stepping out smartly and, as Gillray explained in the caption, "bearing the Sword of Justice," which is coated with blood.

The drawing sent Napoleon into a fury. He instructed Fouché to imprison, without benefit of trial, anyone caught trying to smuggle copies of it into France. He lodged a formal diplomatic complaint against Gillray through his ambassador in London and vowed that if he were ever to succeed in invading England, he would personally go looking for the artist. The reaction was characteristic of the Emperor: when negotiating the Treaty of Amiens with England in 1802, Napoleon had attempted to insert a clause stipulating that all British caricaturists who drew him should be treated in the manner of murderers and forgers, who were subject to extradition and prosecution in France. The English negotiators, puzzled by the request, rejected the amendment.

2.

Louis-Philippe and Napoleon would likely not have responded so vehemently if humour were just a game. In fact, as humourists and their targets have long recognised, jokes are an enormously effective means of anchoring a criticism. At base, they are another way of complaining: about arrogance, cruelty or pomposity, about departures from virtue or good sense.

The most subversive comedy of all may be that which communicates a lesson while seeming only to entertain. Talented comics never deliver sermons outlining abuses of power; instead, they provoke their audiences to acknowledge in a chuckle the aptness of their complaints against authority.

Furthermore (the imprisonment of Philipon notwithstanding), the apparent innocence of jokes enables comics to convey with impunity messages that might be dangerous or impossible to state directly. Historically, for example, court jesters could poke fun at royals over serious matters that could never even be alluded to by other courtiers. (When King James I of England, who presided over

a notoriously corrupt clergy, had trouble fattening up one of his horses, Archibald Armstrong, the court fool, is said to have advised him that all he had to do was make the creature a bishop, and it would rapidly gain the necessary pounds.) Noting the same impulse in his *Jokes and Their Relationship to the Unconscious* (1905), Freud wrote, "A joke will allow us to exploit something ridiculous in our enemy which we could not, on account of obstacles in the way, bring forward openly or consciously." Through jokes, Freud suggested, critical messages "can gain a reception with the hearer which they would never have found in a non-joking form . . . [which is why] jokes are especially favoured in order to make criticism possible against persons in exalted positions."

That said, not every exalted person is ripe for the comic plucking. We rarely laugh, after all, at a doctor who is performing an impor-

James Gillray, The Grand Coronation Procession of Napoleone the 1st Emperor of France, *1805*

tant surgical operation. Yet we may smile at a surgeon who, *after* a hard day in the operating room, returns home and tries to intimidate his wife and daughters by talking to them in pompous medical jargon. We laugh at what is outsized and disproportionate. We laugh at kings whose self-image has outgrown their worth, whose goodness has not kept up with their power; we laugh at high-status individuals who have forgotten their humanity and begun abusing their privileges. We laugh at, and through our laughter criticise, evidence of injustice and excess.

At the hands of the best comics, laughter hence acquires a moral purpose, jokes become attempts to cajole others into reforming their character and habits. Jokes are a way of sketching a political ideal, of creating a more equitable and saner world. Wherever there is inequity or delusion, space opens up for humour-clad criticisms. As Samuel Johnson saw it, satire is only another method, and a particularly effectual one, of "censuring wickedness or folly." In the words of John Dryden, "The true end of satire is the amendment of vices."

3.

History reveals no shortage of jokes intended to amend the vices of high-status groups and shake the mighty out of their pretensions or dishonesty.

In late-eighteenth-century England, for instance, it became fashionable for wealthy young women to wear colossal wigs. Cartoonists offended by the absurdity of the trend quickly produced drawings that amounted to a safe vehicle for urging these ladies to come to their senses—a message that, as Freud would recognise, would have been risky to convey explicitly, given that the wig-wearers owned, or were related or married to men who owned, large tracts of the realm.

At the same time, a fashion for breast-feeding took hold among high-society women, a group who had never before concerned

Engraving from the Oxford Magazine, *1771*

James Gillray, The Fashionable Mamma, *1796*

themselves with babies who now insisted on suckling their infants in order to fit in with progressive notions regarding motherhood. Women who hardly knew where the nursery was in their own house began compulsively exposing their breasts, often between courses at luncheons and dinners. Once again, the cartoonists stepped in to call for moderation.

By the second half of the nineteenth century, yet another affected habit had seized the English upper classes, whose members took to speaking French, especially in restaurants, to demonstrate their intel-

SCENE - *A Restaurant near Leicester Square.*
Jones. " Oh - er - Garsong, regardez eecee - er - apportez - voo le - la - "
Waiter. " Beg pardon, Sir. I don't know French ! "
Jones. " Then for goodness' sake, send me Somebody who *does* ! "

Illustration from Punch, *1895*

lect and eminence. The editors of *Punch* saw in the trend a fresh vice to amend.

A century later in the United States, there was more than enough "wickedness and folly" among Manhattan's elite to keep the cartoonists of the *New Yorker* occupied. In business, many chief executives had a new interest in seeming friendly to their employees—*seeming* being, unfortunately, the operative word here. Instead of changing many of their more brutal practices, they contented themselves with camouflaging them with bland technocratic language, which they hoped might lend some respectability to an exploitation not so very different from that perpetrated by the satanic mills of old. The cartoonists, though, were not fooled. At heart, business remained

Slave galley: "Human resources"

committed to a starkly utilitarian view of employees, wherein any genuine, rather than ritualistic, talk of those employees' fulfilment, or of their employers' responsibilities to them, was tantamount to heresy.

So great were the demands of business that many high-ranking executives, particularly lawyers, permitted the clinically efficient mind-set of their jobs to permeate all areas of their lives, usually at the expense of any spontaneity or sympathy.

"You know what I think folks?
What's important is to be warm, decent human beings . . ."

"I consider myself a passionate man, but a lawyer first."

*"Joyce, I'm so madly in love with you,
I can't eat etc. but that's not why I called . . ."*

Meanwhile, a military class was enjoying unparalleled prestige based on its power to destroy the globe. Cartoonists encouraged their audiences to smile critically at the deathly serious demeanour of the generals.

4.

Beyond being a useful weapon with which to attack the high-status of others, humour may also help us to make sense of, and perhaps even mitigate, our own status anxieties.

A great deal of what we find funny has to do with situations or feelings that, were we to experience them in our own, ordinary lives, would likely cause us either embarrassment or shame. The greatest comics shine a spotlight on vulnerabilities that the rest of us are all too eager to leave in the shadow; they pull us out of our lonely relationship with our most awkward sides. The more private the flaw and the more intense the worry about it, the greater the possibility of laughter—laughter being, in the end, a tribute to the skill with which the unmentionable has been skewered.

Unsurprisingly, therefore, much humour comprises an attempt to name, and thereby contain, anxiety over status. Comedy reassures us that there are others in the world no less envious or socially fragile than ourselves; that other fellow spirits wake up in the early hours feeling every bit as tormented by their financial performance as we

"Which Microsoft Millionaire are you thinking about now?"

*"I usually wake up screaming at six-thirty,
and I'm in the office by nine."*

do by our own; and that beneath the sober appearance society demands of us, most of us are daily going a little bit out of our minds, which in itself should give us cause to hold out a hand to our comparably tortured neighbours.

Rather than *mocking* us for being so concerned with status, the kindest comics *tease* us: they criticise us while simultaneously implying that our basic selves are essentially acceptable. If they are both acute and tactful enough, we may acknowledge with an openhearted laugh bitter truths about ourselves from which we might have recoiled in anger or hurt had they been levelled at us in an ordinary—which is to say, accusatory—way.

5.

Comics, no less than other artists, hence fit rewardingly into Matthew Arnold's definition of art as a discipline offering criticism of life. Their work strives to correct both the injustices of power and the excesses of our envy of those positioned above us in the social hierarchy. Like tragedians, they are motivated by some of the most regrettable aspects of the human condition.

The underlying, unconscious aim of comics may be to bring about, through the adroit use of humour, a world in which there will be a few less things for us to laugh about.

"Of course they're clever. They have to be clever. They haven't got any money."

III
POLITICS

Ideal Human Types

1.

Every society holds certain groups of people in high esteem while condemning or ignoring others, whether on the basis of their skills, accent, temperament, gender, physical attributes, ancestry, religion or skin colour. Yet such arbitrary and subjective criteria for success and failure are far from permanent or universal. Qualities and abilities that equate with high status in one place or era have a marked tendency to grow irrelevant or even become undesirable in others.

A shaft sunk into selected strata of history reveals a catholic range of what different societies in different ages have chosen to regard as honourable traits.

Requirements of High Status In:

Sparta, Greek Peninsula, 400 B.C.
The most honoured members of ancient Spartan society were men—more particularly, aggressive men with large muscles, vigourous (bi)sexual appetites, scant interest in family life, a distaste for business and luxury and an enthusiasm for killing (especially Athenians) on the battlefield. The fighters of Sparta never used money; they avoided hairdressers and entertainers; and they were unsentimental about their wives and children, if they had them. It was a disgrace for such a man ever to be seen in the marketplace; indeed, even knowing how to count was frowned upon, as an indicator of a commercial bent. From the age of seven, every male Spartan was required to train as a soldier, sleep and eat in barracks, and practise battle manoeuvres. Marriage was no impediment: husbands, too, had to live in the barracks, though they were allowed to spend

one night a month with their wives in order to perpetuate their kind. Weak and defective infants were commonly taken out to the barren slopes of Mount Taygetus and left there to die of exposure.

Western Europe, A.D. 476–1096

In many parts of Europe, following the collapse of the western Roman Empire, the most revered individuals were those who modelled their behaviour on the life and teachings of Jesus Christ. These saints, as the Catholic Church deemed them, refused to take up arms, never killed other human beings and tried not to kill animals, either (like many saints, Bernard was a vegetarian; he is even said to have walked very slowly, keeping his eyes on the ground, so as not to step on ants, for they were God's creatures, too). Saints shunned material goods; they did not own horses or property. For Saint Hilarion, home was a cell measuring five feet by four. Saint Francis of Assisi claimed to be married to "Lady Poverty" when he and his followers lived in wattle-and-daub huts, had no tables or chairs and slept on the floor. Saint Anthony of Padua ate only roots and grasses. Saint Dominic de Guzman averted his eyes when he passed the houses of rich merchants.

Saints strove to suppress whatever sexual feelings they may have had and were noted for their extreme physical modesty. Saint Casimir sent away a virgin planted in his bed by his family. Saint Thomas Aquinas is said to have been locked up in a tower with a woman who attempted to use her beauty and perfumes to seduce him; though momentarily aroused, he ultimately abstained and accepted from God a "girdle of perpetual virginity."

Western Europe, circa 1096–1500

In the period after the First Crusade, it was the turn of knights to become the most admired people in Western European society. Knights came from wealthy families; they lived in castles, slept in beds, ate meat and saw nothing wrong in killing those they thought un-Christian (especially Muslims). When they were not killing people, they turned their attention to animals: John de Grailly, for example, boasted of slaughtering four thousand wild boars. Knights were accomplished lovers, too, and wooed women at court, often through the skilful use of poetry. They prized virgins most of all. They were interested in money, but only when it came from land, not through trade. They also liked horses: "Knights have not been chosen to ride an ass or a mule," explained Gutierre Diaz de Gamez (1379–1450), author of *The Unconquered Knight* (circa 1431). "Knights do not come from among feeble or timid or cowardly souls, but from among men who are strong and full of energy, bold and without fear, and for this reason there is no other beast that so befits a knight as a good horse."

England, 1750–1890

In England, by 1750, knowing how to fight was no longer a prerequisite to respectability; more important was knowing how to *dance.* Status now belonged almost exclusively to "gentlemen." Well off and not expected to do much more than preside over the management of their estates, they might dabble in industry or trade (particularly with India and the West Indies) but should by no means allow themselves to be confused with the inferior caste of merchants and industrialists. They were supposed to like their families and refrain from leaving their children on hillsides to die. At the same time, it was perfectly all right for them to keep mistresses in town.

Much emphasis was placed on the cultivation of a certain languid elegance. It was important to take care of one's hair and to visit a barber regularly. Lord Chesterfield, in his *Letters to His Son* (1751), advised that a gentleman's conversation should be free of any "misplaced eagerness" that might result in the repetition of "trifling or ill-timed anecdotes with silly preambles like 'I will tell you an excellent thing.'" Chesterfield also stressed that a gentleman ought to be able to execute a decent minuet: "Remember that the graceful motion of the arms, the giving of your hand, and the putting-on and putting-off of your hat genteelly are the material parts of a gentleman's dancing." As for relations with the opposite sex, a gentleman was meant to marry, while bearing in mind that (in Chesterfield's words) "women are only children of a larger growth." If seated next to one at dinner, a gentleman was to "prattle" on to her rather than hold his tongue, lest she mistake his silence for dullness or arrogance.

Brazil, 1600–1960
Among the Cubeo tribe of the northwestern Amazon, the highest rung on the social ladder was reserved for men who spoke very little (for babbling was thought to sap strength), and did not partake in dancing or in raising children but were instead, first and foremost, skilled at killing jaguars. Whereas low-status men were limited to fishing, high-status individuals went hunting. Anyone who killed a jaguar would wear its teeth on a necklace, and the more jaguars one could claim as trophies, the better one's chances of becoming the "headman" or tribal chief. Headmen wore large jaguar-tooth necklaces as well as armadillo girdles. The women of the tribe were meanwhile relegated to growing manioc root in jungle clearings. Few things could bring more shame on a man than being seen helping his wife prepare a root-based meal.

2.
What are the principles according to which status is distributed? Why is it that military men are applauded in one society, and landed gentry in another? At least four answers suggest themselves.

The members of a group may acquire status by threatening to

harm others physically, thus bullying a population into offering its respect.

Alternatively, certain people may win status through their ability to defend others, whether by strength, by patronage or through control of food, water and other staples. Where safety is in short supply, as in ancient Sparta or twelfth-century Europe, courageous fighters and knights on horseback will be celebrated. If a community craves nutrients that are available only in the form of elusive animal flesh, as in the Amazon, it is the killers of jaguars who will earn respect and its symbol, the armadillo girdle. In areas where the livelihood of the majority depends on trade and high technology, as in modern Europe and North America, entrepreneurs and scientists will be the objects of admiration. The converse also holds true: a segment of the population that cannot provide a useful service to others will end up without status, in the manner of muscular men in countries with secure borders, or of jaguar hunters in settled agricultural societies.

Elevated status may also be accorded to those who impress others with their goodness, physical talents, artistic skills or wisdom, as happened with saints in Christian Europe and occurs with European footballers today.

Finally, a group may appeal to the conscience or sense of decency of its peers, and so eloquently articulate the justice of its cause that the sheer weight of its moral authority will tip the balance of status towards a redistribution in its favour.

As the determinants of high status keep shifting, so, too, naturally, will the triggers of status anxiety be altered. Within one group, we may have to worry about our ability to launch a spear into the flank of a moving target, within another about our prowess on the battlefield, within a third about our capacity for devotion to God and within yet a fourth about having what it takes to wrest a profit from the capital markets.

3.

For those made most anxious or embittered by the ideals of their own societies, the history of status, even crudely outlined, cannot but reveal a basic and inspiring point: ideals are not cast in stone. Status values have long been, and in the future may again be, subject to alteration. And the word we might use to describe this process of change is *politics.*

By waging political battle, different groups may always attempt to transform the honour systems of their communities and win dignity for themselves over the opposition of all those with a stake in the prior arrangement. Through a ballot box, a gun, a strike or sometimes even a book, these factions will strive to redirect their societies' notions of who is rightfully owed the privileges that accompany high status.

A Political Perspective on Modern Status Anxiety

1.

If a talent for hunting jaguars, dancing a minuet, riding a horse in battle or imitating the life of Christ no longer offers sufficient cause to be labelled a success, what, then, may be said to constitute the dominant contemporary Western ideal according to which people are judged and status is allotted?

We may, without making any scientific claims for the portrait, sketch at least some of the concerns and qualities of our own day's prototypical success story, the inheritor of the high status variously claimed, in the past, by the warrior, the saint, the knight and the aristocratic landed gentleman.

Requirements of High Status in:

London, New York, Los Angeles, Sydney, 2004
A successful person may be a man or a woman, of any race, who has been able to accumulate money, power and renown through his or her own accomplishments (rather than through inheritance) in one of the myriad sectors of the commercial world (including sport, art and scientific research). Because societies are in practise trusted to be "meritocratic," financial achievements are necessarily understood to be "deserved." The ability to accumulate wealth is prized as proof of the presence of at least four cardinal virtues: creativity, courage, intelligence and stamina. The presence or absence of other virtues— humility and godliness, for example—rarely detains attention. That success is no longer attributed, as in past societies, to "luck," "providence" or "God" is a reflection of the collective secular faith we now place in individual will power. Financial failures are judged to be

similarly merited, with unemployment's bearing some of the shame that physical cowardice earned in warrior eras. Money is meanwhile invested with an ethical quality. Its relative quantity indicates the virtue of its possessor, as do the material goods it can buy. Like the Cubeo's necklace of jaguar teeth, a prosperous way of life signals worthiness, while ownership of a rusted old car or a threadbare home may prompt suppositions of moral deficiency. Aside from its promise of high status, wealth is promoted on the basis of its capacity to deliver happiness by granting access to an array of ever-changing conveniences and luxuries, the thought of whose absence in the restricted lives of previous generations can invoke pity and wonder.

2.

However natural such a status ideal may appear to be, it is, of course—as a well-considered political perspective must show—only the work of humans, a recent development dating from the middle of the eighteenth century, brought into being by a host of identifiable factors. Furthermore, the political perspective would add, as an ideal, it is occasionally simpleminded, at times unfair and always subject to change.

No aspect of this peculiar modern ideal has come under greater scrutiny than the associations it constructs between, on the one hand, wealth and virtue and, on the other, poverty and moral dubiousness. In *The Theory of the Leisure Class* (1899), Thorstein Veblen considered the emergence of financial worth, in the early nineteenth century, as the central and often sole criterion employed in commercial societies' evaluation of their members: "[Wealth has become] the conventional basis of esteem. Its possession has become necessary in order to have any reputable standing in the community. It has become indispensable to acquire property in order to retain one's good name . . . Those members of the community who fall short of [a relatively high standard of wealth] will suffer in the esteem of their fellow men; and consequently they will suffer also in their own esteem." In such a society, it was, Veblen implied, nearly impossible to conceive of being both virtuous *and yet* poor. Even the most unmaterialistically minded person must sense an imperative to accumulate wealth and demonstrate possession of it—as the only means of escaping opprobrium—and must feel anxious and blameworthy on failing to do so.

Accordingly, the possession of a great many material goods becomes desirable not principally because such goods provide any abjective or subjective pleasure (though they may do this, too) but because they confer honour. In the ancient world, debate raged among philosophers about what was materially necessary for happiness and what unnecessary. Epicurus, for one, argued that simple food and shelter were all that was needed, and that an expensive house and lavish meals could be safely passed up by every rational, philosophically minded person. However, reviewing the argument many centuries later in *The Wealth of Nations,* Adam Smith wryly pointed out that in modern, materialistic societies, countless things that were no doubt unnecessary from the point of view of physical survival had nonetheless in practical terms come to be seen as "necessaries," simply because no one could be thought respectable and so lead a psychologically comfortable life without owning them:

"By necessaries I understand not only the commodities which are indispensably necessary for the support of life, but whatever the custom of the country renders it indecent for creditable people, even of the lowest order, to be without. A linen shirt, for example, is, strictly speaking, not a necessary of life. The Greeks and Romans lived, I suppose, very comfortably though they had no linen. But in the present times, through the greater part of Europe, a creditable daylabourer would be ashamed to appear in public without a linen shirt, the want of which would be supposed to denote that disgraceful degree of poverty which, it is presumed, nobody can well fall into without extreme bad conduct.... Under necessaries, therefore, I comprehend not only those things which nature, but those things which the established rules of decency[,] have rendered necessary to the lowest rank of people."

Since Smith's day, economists have been almost unanimous in subscribing to the idea that what best defines, and lends such bitterness to, the condition of the poor is not so much the direct physical suffering involved as the shame attendant on the negative reactions of others to their state—in other words, the unavoidable sense that their poverty flouts what Smith termed the "established rules of decency." In *The Affluent Society* (1958), J. K. Galbraith proposed, with a bow to Smith, "People are poverty-stricken whenever their income, even if adequate for survival, falls markedly behind that of the community. Then they cannot have what the larger community regards as the minimum necessary for decency; and they cannot wholly escape, therefore, the judgment of the larger community that they are indecent."

3.

This notion that "decency" must be attached to wealth—and "indecency" to poverty—is the essential focal point of one line of sceptical complaint against the modern status ideal. Why, the system's critics ask, should a failure to pile up riches be taken as a marker of an unconditionally flawed human being, rather than evidence of a greater or lesser deficit, or even a fiasco, in one particular aspect of the far larger, more complicated project that is the leading of a good life? Why should wealth and poverty be read as unerring signposts for human morals?

The reasons, it turns out, are not mysterious. The very act of earn-

ing money frequently calls upon virtues of character. Working at—
and keeping—almost any job requires intelligence, energy, fore-
thought and the ability to cooperate with others. And the more
lucrative the position, the greater the requisite merits. Lawyers and
surgeons not only earn higher salaries than street cleaners; they also
typically bring to bear on their work more sustained effort and
greater skill.

A day labourer "would be ashamed to appear in public without a
linen shirt," wrote Adam Smith, because (to return to his passage
with italics) not having such a shirt must imply a degree of poverty
that, Smith's contemporaries felt certain, "*nobody can well fall into
without extreme bad conduct.*" Only someone who was a congenital
drunk, unreliable, thieving or childishly insubordinate would be
incapable of securing the modest employment needed to finance the
purchase of a linen shirt—given which, the ownership of this article
of clothing might indeed safely be taken as a minimum guarantee of
good character.

It requires but a short leap of imagination from there to make the
assumption that *extreme good conduct* and an assortment of virtues
must lie behind the acquisition of cupboards full of linen shirts,
fleets of yachts, myriad mansions and jewels. The very concept of the
"status symbol," a costly material object that confers respect on its
owner, rests upon the widespread and not improbable notion that
the acquisition of the most expensive goods must inevitably demand
the greatest of all qualities of character.

4.

Opponents of economic meritocracy have long believed, however,
that true merit must be a more elusive, complex quality than could
ever be neatly captured by the parameters of an end-of-year salary.
Their scepticism is analogous to that of educationalists who insist

that the "intelligence" of students cannot be fairly measured simply by making them sit an examination and then grading their answers to questions such as:

Pick out the antonyms from among these four words:
    obdurate   spurious   ductile   recondite

For the most part these critics would not argue, of course, that merit and intelligence are, respectively, everywhere equally distributed or entirely immeasurable. They merely wish to point out that the vast majority of us are unlikely ever to know how to do the apportioning or measuring properly and hence should take infinite care before acting in ways that presume otherwise—for example, in the economic sphere, by abolishing taxes for the wealthy (who, it is occasionally said by extreme defenders of economic meritocracy, deserve to keep all their earnings) or revoking state benefits for the poor (who would thus, these same defenders would add, have the opportunity more fully to experience the depths of deprivation that they must likewise deserve).

Such scepticism does not sit well, though, with the demands of everyday life. It is easy to understand the wish for some system, be it educational or economic, that will assure us of picking out the worthiest few from a classroom or in society and, in turn, passing over the least worthy—that is, the losers—*in good conscience.*

But an urgent wish is no guarantor of a sound solution. In *The Intelligent Woman's Guide to Socialism and Capitalism* (1928), George Bernard Shaw concluded that modern capitalist societies had settled on a particularly obtuse means of determining the economic hierarchy: a system whose basic tenet was that "if every man is left to make as much money as he can for himself in his own way, subject only to the laws restraining crude violence and direct fraud, then wealth will spontaneously distribute itself in proportion to the industry, sobriety and generally the virtue of the citizens, the good men becoming rich and the bad men poor."

Quite to the contrary, continued Shaw, it had been demonstrated all too clearly that under capitalism, any ruthless, ambitious man could "grab three or four million pounds for himself by selling bad whiskey or by forestalling the wheat harvest and selling it at three times its cost or by running silly newspapers and magazines that circulate deceitful advertisements," even as decent "men who exercise[d] their noble faculties or risk[ed] their lives in the furtherance of human knowledge and welfare" ended up mired in poverty and insignificance.

That said, Shaw did not want to align himself with those sentimental types on the left and the right who liked to claim that in society as it was presently arranged, it was always the good men who became poor and the bad men rich—a formula no less simplistic than its inverse. He sought rather to invoke in his readers a sense of how limiting it was to try to judge anyone morally on the basis of salary, and how much nobler to take some account of the many consequences that might result from differences in wealth.

In *Unto This Last* (1862), John Ruskin, as intent as Shaw would later be on challenging meritocratic ideas, related in heavily sarcastic terms the conclusions he had reached regarding the characters of the rich and the poor, after hundreds of encounters with representatives of both groups in many countries over four decades: "The persons who become rich are, generally speaking, industrious, resolute, proud, covetous, prompt, methodical, sensible, unimaginative, insensitive and ignorant. The persons who remain poor are the entirely foolish, the entirely wise, the idle, the reckless, the humble, the thoughtful, the dull, the imaginative, the sensitive, the well-informed, the improvident, the irregularly and impulsively wicked, the clumsy knave, the open thief and the entirely merciful just and godly person." In other words, in Ruskin's experience, there was no classifying those who ended up either rich *or* poor—which means for us, if we follow the message first articulated by Jesus Christ and subsequently repeated in a secular idiom by political thinkers across the nineteenth and twentieth centuries, that it is not our prerogative to ascribe honour principally according to income. A multitude of external events and internal characteristics will go into making one person wealthy and another destitute, among them luck and circumstance, illness and fear, accident and late development, good timing and misfortune.

Three centuries before Ruskin and Shaw, Michel de Montaigne had similarly stressed the importance of contingent factors in determining the outcome of lives. He advised us to remember the role played by "chance in bestowing glory on us according to her fickle will: I have often seen chance marching ahead of merit, and often outstripping merit by a long chalk." A dispassionate audit of our successes and failures should leave us feeling that there are reasons to be at once less proud of and less embarrassed about ourselves, for a thought-provoking percentage of what happens to us is not of our own doing. Montaigne urged that we keep a tight rein on our excitement when meeting the powerful and wealthy, and on our tendency to judge in the presence of the poor and obscure. "A man may have a great suite of attendants, a beautiful palace, great influence and a large income. All that may *surround* him, but it is not *in* him. . . . Measure his height with his stilts off: let him lay aside his wealth and his decorations and show himself to us naked. . . . What sort of soul does he have? Is his soul a beautiful one, able, happily endowed with all her functions? Are her riches her own or are they borrowed? Has luck had nothing to do with it? . . . That is what we need to know; that is what the immense distances between us men should be judged by."

Uniting the many challenges to the commercial meritocratic ideal is a threefold plea, that we cease investing with moral connotations something as apparently haphazardly distributed as money; that we sever the doctrinaire connections routinely made between wealth and virtue; and that before we begin measuring our peers, we at least attempt to ensure that the taller ones have taken off their stilts, and that the shorter ones are not standing in a ditch.

5.

Aside from the equation it draws between making money and being good, the modern ideal of a successful life posits a further linkage between making money and being happy.

This latter association rests on three assumptions. First, it is presumed that identifying what will make us happy is not an inordinately difficult task. Just as our bodies typically know what they need in order to be healthy, and hence direct us towards smoked fish, say, when we lack sodium or towards peaches when our blood sugar is low, so, too, the theory goes, can our minds be relied upon to understand what we should aim for so as to flourish as whole human beings. They will thus naturally push us towards certain careers and projects. Second, it is taken for granted that the enormous range of occupational possibilities and consumer goods available to modern civilisation is not merely a gaudy, enervating show responsible for stoking desires bearing little relevance to our welfare but is, rather, a helpful array of potentialities and products capable of satisfying some of our most important needs. And third, conventional wisdom holds that the more money we have, the more goods and services we will be able to afford, thus increasing our odds of being happy.

The most suggestive and readable adversary of these several assumptions remains Jean-Jacques Rousseau, most forcefully in his *Discourse on the Origin of Inequality* (1754). In this text, Rousseau begins by charging that however independent-minded we may believe ourselves to be, we are in fact dangerously inept at deciphering our own needs. Our souls rarely articulate what they must have in order to be fulfilled, and when they do manage to mumble something, their requests are likely to be misfounded or contradictory. Rather than compare the mind with a body that is unfailingly correct in its sense of what it ought to consume for its own health, Rousseau invites us to draw an analogy instead to a body that cries out for wine when it needs water and insists that it wants to dance when it should in truth be lying flat on a bed. Our minds are susceptible to the influence of external voices telling us what we require to be satisfied, voices that may drown out the faint sounds emitted by our souls and distract us from the careful, arduous task of accurately naming our priorities.

Rousseau's *Discourse* goes on to sketch the history of the world not as a story of progress from barbarism to the great workshops and cities of Europe, but as one of regress, from a privileged state in which we humans lived simply but were aware of our own needs to a state in which we are apt to feel envy for ways of life that can claim little connection to our true selves. In technologically backward prehistory, in Rousseau's "natural state," when people lived in forests and had never entered a shop or read a newspaper, men and women alike better understood themselves and so were drawn towards the more essential features of a happy life: love of family, respect for nature, awe at the beauty of the universe, curiosity about others and a taste for music and humble entertainments. It was from this state that modern commercial "civilisation" pulled us, according to the philosopher, leaving us to envy and yearn and suffer in a world of plenty.

For the benefit of those who might wish to explain this away as the absurdly romantic fantasy of a pastoral author unreasonably offended by modernity, it is worth noting here that if the eighteenth century paid attention to Rousseau's argument, it was in part because it had before it a single, stark example of its evident truths, in the fate of the indigenous populations of North America.

Reports of Native American society dating from the sixteenth century describe it as a materially modest yet psychologically rewarding culture: communities were small, close-knit, egalitarian, religious, playful and martial. The Indians were certainly backward in the commercial and financial sense: they lived on a diet of fruits and wild animals, slept in tepees and had few possessions. Year after year, they wore the same pelts and shoes. Even a chief might own no more than a spear and a few pots. But there was reputed to be an impressive level of contentment amid the simplicity.

Within only a few decades of the arrival of the first Europeans, however, the status system of Native American society would be turned on its head through contact with the products of European technology and industry. What mattered most was no longer an individual's wisdom or understanding of the ways of nature, but his ownership of weapons, jewellery and whiskey. Indians now longed for silver earrings, copper and brass bracelets, tin finger rings, necklaces made of Venetian glass, ice chisels, guns, alcohol, kettles, beads, hoes and mirrors.

These new enthusiasms did not develop spontaneously. European traders deliberately sought to foster desires in the Indians in order to motivate them to provide the animal pelts required by the European market. By 1690, an English naturalist, the Reverend John Banister, could note that the Indians of the Hudson Bay area had been successfully tempted by traders to want "many things which they had not wanted before, because they never had them, but which by means of trade are now highly necessary to them." Two decades later, a traveller named Robert Beverley observed, "The Europeans have introduced luxury among the Indians which has multiplied their wants and made them desire a thousand things they never even dreamt of before."

Unfortunately, these thousand things, however ardently coveted, did not seem to make the Indians much happier. Without question, they worked harder: between 1739 and 1759, for example, the two thousand warriors of the Cherokee tribe were estimated to have killed 1.25 million deer to satisfy export demands. During the same period, the Montagnais Indians on the northern shore of the Saint Lawrence River turned over between twelve thousand and fifteen thousand pelts a year to French and British merchants at Tadoussac. But their quality of life did not improve as the volume of trade increased. Suicide and alcoholism rates rose, communities were fractured and factions squabbled among themselves over the European booty. The tribal chiefs did not need Rousseau's commentary to understand what had happened, though they unknowingly concurred with his analysis. There were calls for the Indians to renounce their addiction to European "luxuries." In the 1760s, the leaders of the Delaware tribes of western Pennsylvania and the Ohio Valley tried to revive the ways of their forefathers. Prophecies warned that the Delaware would be wiped out if they did not wean themselves from their dependence on trade. But already it was too late: the Indians, no different in their psychological makeup from other humans, had succumbed to the easy lure of the trinkets of modern civilisation and ceased listening to the quiet voices inside, which spoke of the modest pleasures of the community and the beauty of the empty canyons at dusk.

6.

The defenders of commercial society have always had one answer for those sympathetic to the American Indians, and for anyone else who thought to complain of the corrupting effects of an advanced economy: no one *forced* the Indians to buy necklaces made of Venetian glass, ice chisels, guns, kettles, beads, hoes or mirrors. No one stopped them from living in tepees and made them aspire to owning wooden houses with porches and wine cellars. The Indians abandoned their sober, simple ways of their own accord—which in itself might indicate, this line of reasoning holds, that theirs was perhaps not as pleasant a life as has been made out.

The defence is similar to that embraced by modern advertising agents and newspaper editors, who are fond of asserting that *they* are not the ones responsible for encouraging the public's undue obsession with the lives of the famous, changes in fashion or the ownership of new products. No, they merely offer up information related to these topics for anyone who may be interested—while, the implication goes, many more may prefer to help the needy, examine their own souls, read Edward Gibbon's *Decline and Fall* or reflect upon the short passage of time left to them before their extinction.

This response illuminates why Rousseau placed so much emphasis, unedifying though it might be, on how difficult humans find it to make up their minds about what is important, and how strongly predisposed they are to listen to others' suggestions about where their thoughts should be directed and what they should value in order to be happy. Such suggestions evidently carry even greater weight when they appear on newsprint or in giant type on a billboard.

The great irony here is that it should be the advertising agents and newspaper editors themselves who are typically the first to downplay the effectiveness of their own trades. They will insist that the population is independent-minded enough not to be overly affected by the stories they lay before the world, nor taken in for long by the siren call of the adverts they so artfully design.

In protesting thus they are, sadly, being far too modest. Nothing more clearly illustrates the extent of their deprecation than a statisti-

Percentage of North Americans Declaring
the Following Items to Be Necessities

	1970	2000
Second car	20	59
Second television set	3	45
More than one telephone	2	78
Car air conditioning	11	65
Home air conditioning	22	70
Dishwasher	8	44

cal glimpse of the speed with which what was once a mere possibility will, given sufficient prompting, come to seem a necessity.

Criticisms of consumer society have focused not only on the shortcomings and inadequacies of products in general (a point open to overelaboration, for it takes a curmudgeonly spirit not to be struck by, say, the softness of a cashmere pullover or the beauty of a car's dashboard on a nighttime drive along a motorway) but also, and more fairly, perhaps, on the distorted picture of our needs created by the way these products are presented to us. They can appear essential, blessed with extraordinary powers to bestow happiness on us, because we understand neither their actual identity nor our own functioning.

A car advertisement will, for example, be careful to ignore aspects of human psychology and of the overall process of buying and owning that could spoil, or at least dampen, our joy at coming to possess the featured vehicle. Most notably, it will fail to mention our ten-

The new SL-Class

FOR SALE:
That recurring dream of yours.

THE NEW SL-CLASS FROM £67,790 ON THE ROAD. CALL 0800 776655 FOR MORE
DETAILS OR VISIT WWW.MERCEDES-BENZ.CO.UK. CAR FEATURED IS AN SL500
WITH OPTIONAL ALLOY WHEELS AT £69,190 ON THE ROAD (INCLUDES DELIVERY,
NUMBER PLATES, FIRST REGISTRATION TAX AND A FULL TANK OF FUEL).

Mercedes-Benz

dency to cease being excited by anything after we have owned it for a short while. The quickest way to stop noticing something, may be to buy it—just as the quickest way to stop appreciating someone may be to marry him or her. We are tempted to believe that certain achievements and possessions will give us enduring satisfaction. We are invited to imagine ourselves scaling the steep cliff face of happiness in order to reach a wide, high plateau on which we will live out

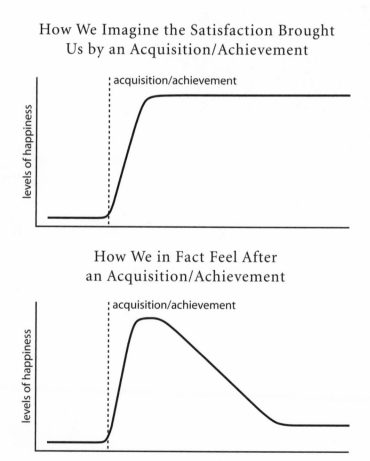

How We Imagine the Satisfaction Brought Us by an Acquisition/Achievement

acquisition/achievement

levels of happiness

How We in Fact Feel After an Acquisition/Achievement

acquisition/achievement

levels of happiness

the rest of our lives; we are not reminded that soon after gaining the summit, we will be called down again into fresh lowlands of anxiety and desire.

Life seems to be a process of replacing one anxiety with another and substituting one desire for another—which is not to say that we should never strive to overcome any of our anxieties or fulfil any of our desires, but rather to suggest that we should perhaps build into our strivings an awareness of the way our goals promise us a respite and a resolution that they cannot, by definition, deliver. The new car will rapidly be absorbed, like all the other wonders we already own, into the material backdrop of our lives, where we will hardly register its existence—until the night when a burglar does us the paradoxical service of smashing a window to steal the radio and brings home to us, in the midst of the shattered glass, how much we had to be grateful for.

The advertisement stays quiet, too, about the relative inability of any material thing to alter our level of happiness, as compared with the overwhelming power of emotional events. The most elegant and accomplished of vehicles cannot give us a fraction of the satisfaction we derive from a good relationship, just as it cannot be of any comfort whatsoever to us following a domestic argument or abandonment. At such moments, we may even come to resent the car's impassive efficiency, the punctilious clicking of its indicators and the methodical calculations of its onboard computer.

We are equally prone to misunderstand the attractions of certain careers, simply because so much of what they entail is always edited out of the description, leaving only highlights that it would be impossible not to admire. We read of the results, not of the labour required to produce them.

If we cannot stop envying, it seems especially poignant that we should be constrained to spend so much of our lives envying the wrong things.

7.

The essence of the charge made against the modern high-status ideal is that it is guilty of effecting a gigantic distortion of priorities, of elevating to the highest level of achievement a process of material accumulation that should instead be only one of many factors determining the direction of our lives under a more truthful, more broadly defined conception of ourselves.

Incensed by their wrongheaded prioritising, John Ruskin excoriated nineteenth-century Britons (he had never been to the United States) for being the most wealth-obsessed people in the history of the world. They were never at any moment, he wrote, free of concern with who had what, and where it had come from ("the ruling goddess may be best generally described as the 'Goddess of Getting-on,'" he grumbled). They felt shame over their own financial state and jealousy towards those whom they perceived as being better off.

Ruskin had a confession to make: contrary to expectations, he, too, felt frantic to become wealthy. The thought of wealth preyed on his mind from breakfast till dinner, he admitted. In fact, however, he was sarcastically playing off an ambiguity in the term *wealth* to emphasise all the more forcefully how far he felt his fellow countrymen had strayed from virtue. For the dictionary tells us that *wealth* refers not only, and historically not even primarily, to large amounts of money; it can denote an abundance of anything, from butterflies to books to smiles. Ruskin *was* interested in wealth—obsessed by it, even—but in wealth of a very different kind than is usually meant by the word: he wished to be wealthy in kindness, curiosity, sensitivity, humility, godliness and intelligence, a set of virtues to which he applied the collective name "life." In *Unto This Last,* he therefore entreated his readers to set aside their ordinary monetary conceptions of wealth in favour of a "life"-based schema, according to which the wealthiest people in Britain would no longer automatically be the merchants and the landowners, but rather those who felt the keenest wonder gazing at the stars at night or who were best able to sense and alleviate the sufferings of others. "There is no wealth but life," he intoned: "life, including all its powers of love, of joy and of admiration. That country is richest which nourishes the greatest number of noble and happy human beings; that man is richest who, having perfected the functions of his own life to the utmost, has also the widest helpful influence, both personal, and by means of his possessions, over the lives of others . . . Many of the persons commonly considered wealthy are, in reality, no more wealthy than the locks of their own strong boxes, they being inherently and eternally incapable of wealth."

Ruskin was here uttering the plain, unsophisticated truths of the prophets, and when people did not guffaw (the *Saturday Review* dismissed the writer as a "mad governess" and his thesis as "windy hysterics," "absolute nonsense" and "intolerable twaddle"), they listened. In 1906, on entering Parliament, Britain's first twenty-seven Labour MPs were asked what single book had most influenced them to pursue social justice through politics. Seventeen of them cited *Unto This Last*. Thirteen years later, George Bernard Shaw, speaking on the centenary of Ruskin's birth, declared that the invective of Vladimir Lenin and the indictments of Karl Marx, when compared with Ruskin's works, sounded more like the platitudes of a rural dean. (Ruskin himself, however, because he enjoyed teasing label-fixers, had claimed to be a "violent Tory of the old school—Walter Scott's school, that is to say, and Homer's"). "I have met in my lifetime some extremely revolutionary characters," Shaw went on, "and quite a large number of them, when I have asked, 'Who put you on to this revolutionary line? Was it Marx?' have answered plainly, 'No, it was Ruskin.' Ruskinites are perhaps the most thorough-going of all the opponents of the existing state of our society. Ruskin's political message to the cultured people of his day, the class to which he himself belonged, began and ended in this simple judgement: 'You are a parcel of thieves.'"

Ruskin was not alone in holding this opinion. There were others in the nineteenth century who hammered home, in tones alternately outraged and melancholy, identical criticisms of money's deification as the chief determinant of respect, a presumed badge of demonstrable goodness, rather than merely one component, and surely not the most important one, of a fulfilled and fulfilling life. "Men are always apt to regard wealth as a precious end in itself and certainly they have never been so apt thus to regard it as they are in England at the present time," lamented Matthew Arnold in *Culture and Anarchy* (1869). "Never did people believe anything more firmly, than nine Englishmen out of ten at the present day believe that our greatness and welfare are proved by our being so very rich." As Ruskin had done seven years before, Arnold urged the inhabitants of the world's first and most advanced industrial nation to think of wealth as only one of many means to secure happiness, an end that he defined (to further hoots of laughter from critics at the *Daily Telegraph*) as an "inward spiritual activity, having for its characters increased sweetness, increased light, increased life and increased sympathy."

Thomas Carlyle had earlier made much the same point, if less diplomatically. In *Midas* (1843), he asked, "This successful industry of England, with its plethoric wealth . . . which of us has it enriched? . . . We have sumptuous garnitures for our life, but have forgotten to *live* in the middle of them. Many men eat finer cookery, drink dearer liquors, but in the heart of them, what increase of blessedness is there? Are they better, beautifuller, stronger, braver? Are they even what they call 'happier'? Do they look with satisfaction on more things and human faces in this God's Earth; do more things and human faces look with satisfaction on them? Not so . . . We have profoundly forgotten everywhere that cash-payment is not the sole relation of human beings."

Carlyle was not blind to the benefits of modern enterprise; he even saw the appeal of certain aspects of accountancy ("book-keeping by double-entry is admirable, and records several things in an exact manner," he conceded). But like Arnold and Ruskin and any number of other social critics before them and since, he could not accept a way of life in which what he termed "Mammon-worship" had apparently subsumed the drive towards "blessedness" and "satisfaction" on "God's Earth."

Political Change

1.

However disgruntled or puzzled a social hierarchy may leave us feeling, we are apt to go along with it on the resigned assumption that it is too entrenched and must be too well founded to be questioned. We are led to believe, in other words, that communities and the principles underpinning them are, practically speaking, immutable— even, somehow, *natural.*

2.

Many distinctive ideas have, over the course of history, been thought of as "natural." Some of the most peculiar of these flourished in the late nineteenth and early twentieth centuries:

The real fact is that man in the beginning was ordained to rule over woman: and this is an eternal decree which we have no right and no power to alter.

EARL PERCY, 1873

There is more difference, physically and morally, between an educated European man and a European woman than there is between a European man and a negro belonging to some savage Central African tribe.

LORD CROMER, 1911

The majority of women (happily for them) are not very much troubled with sexual feeling of any kind.

SIR WILLIAM ACTON, 1857

As a race the African is inferior to the white man; subordination
to the white man is his normal condition. Therefore our system, which regards the African as an inferior, rests upon a great
law of nature.

ALEXANDER STEPHENS, 1861

3.

Within a given society, political consciousness may be said to emerge
through the realisation that certain opinions paraded as a priori
truths by influential figures may in fact be relative and open to investigation. If they have been declaimed with sufficient confidence,
however, these truisms may seem to belong to the fabric of existence
no less than the trees and the sky, though they have been—a political
perspective insists—wholly invented by individuals with specific
practical and psychological interests to defend.

If such relativity is hard to keep in mind, it may be because dominant beliefs themselves are typically at pains to suggest that they are
no more alterable by human hands than are the orbits of the sun.
They claim to be merely stating the obvious. They are, to use Karl
Marx's helpful word, *ideological*—an ideological statement being
defined as one that subtly promotes a bias while pretending to be
perfectly neutral.

For Marx, it is the ruling classes of a society that will be largely
responsible for disseminating its ideological beliefs. This explains
why, in those societies in which a landed gentry controls the balance
of power, the concept of the inherent nobility of landed wealth is
taken for granted by the majority of the population (including many
who lose out under the system), while in mercantile societies, it is the
achievements of entrepreneurs that dominate the citizenry's con-

cepts of success. As Marx posited, "The ruling ideas of every age are always the ideas of the ruling class."

Yet somewhat paradoxically, these ideas would never come to rule if they were perceived as ruling too forcefully. It is in the perfidious nature of ideological statements that unless our political senses are well developed, we will fail to spot them. Ideology is released into society like a colourless, odourless gas. It pervades newspapers, advertisements, television programmes and textbooks, always making light of its partial, perhaps illogical or unjust take on the world and meekly implying that it is only presenting age-old truths with which none but a fool or a maniac could disagree.

4.

But the nascent political mind casts off politeness and tradition, refuses to blame itself for adopting a contrary stance and asks, with all the innocence of a child and the tenacity of a trial lawyer, "Does this have to be?"

An oppressive situation that might otherwise have been taken as a sign that nature had condemned certain members of society to suffer—and suffer *in perpetuity*—may now, by being reinterpreted politically, be attributed to theoretically changeable social forces. Guilt and shame may thus be transmuted into understanding and a striving towards a more equitable distribution of status.

5.

George Bernard Shaw, *The Intelligent Woman's Guide to Socialism and Capitalism* (London, 1928):
"You must clear your mind of the fancy with which we all begin as children, that the institutions under which we live are natural, like the

weather. They are not. Because they exist everywhere in our little world, we take it for granted that they have always existed and must always exist. That is a dangerous mistake. They are in fact transient makeshifts. Changes that nobody ever believed possible take place in a few generations. Children nowadays believe that to spend nine years at school, to have old-age and widows' pensions, votes for women and short-skirted ladies in Parliament is part of the order of nature and always was and ever will be; but their great-grandmothers would have said that anyone who told them that such things were coming was mad—and that anyone who wanted them to come was wicked."

6.

The segment of Western society that perhaps most successfully altered its status over the course of the twentieth century was women. The manner in which large numbers of them came to feel entitled to question their position in the hierarchy provides a host of general insights into the development of a political consciousness.

Virginia Woolf's *A Room of One's Own* (1929) begins with a description of a visit the author paid one autumn to Cambridge University. While there, she decided to stop in at Trinity College Library and have a look at the manuscripts of Milton's *Lycidas* and Thackeray's *The History of Henry Esmond*. However, just as she was about to step inside, "a deprecating, silvery, kindly gentleman" appeared and "regretted in a low voice that ladies are only admitted to the library if accompanied by a Fellow of the College or furnished with a letter of introduction." In a minor key, Woolf had bumped into one of the great stately pillars that propped up the lesser status of women: disenfranchisement from equal rights to higher education.

Faced with a similar situation, many women would have felt stung, but few would have responded politically to the offence. Most would instead have blamed themselves or nature or God—anything but the social construct that condoned such exclusion. After all, never in history had women had the same rights to education as men. Had not many of the most famous doctors in Britain—and plenty of politicians, too—made reference to the biological inferiority of the female brain, a supposed consequence of the smaller size of women's skulls? What right, then, did any one woman have to question the motives of a gentleman who turned her away from a library, especially if he delivered his message with an apology and a polite smile?

But this particular woman was not to be easily silenced. Performing the quintessential political manoeuvre, she asked herself not, What is wrong with *me* for not being allowed into a library? but rather, What is wrong with *the keepers of the library* for not allowing *me* in? When ideas and institutions are held to be "natural," responsibility for whatever suffering they cause must necessarily belong either to no specific agent or else to the injured parties themselves. But the political perspective gives the oppressed leave to imagine that it might be the ideal, instead of something in their own character, that is at fault. Rather than wonder in shame, What is wrong with *me* (that I am a woman/have dark skin/have no money)? they are encouraged to ask, What might be wrong, unjust or illogical in those *others* who disdain me? And the question may, moreover, be put not out of some conviction of innocence (the stance of those who use political radicalism as a paranoid means of avoiding self-criticism) but in recognition of the fact that there is more folly and partisanship in institutions, ideas and laws than a naturalistic perspective can possibly allow for.

As she made her way back to her Cambridge hotel, Woolf moved outwards from her own hurt to consider the position of women in general: "I pondered what effect poverty has on the mind; and what effect wealth has on the mind and I thought how unpleasant it is to be locked out and of the safety and prosperity of the one sex and the poverty and insecurity of the other." She reflected upon, and began to be sceptical of, the feminine role model she had grown up with: the image of a woman who was at all times, "immensely charming and utterly unselfish. She excelled in the difficult arts of family life. She sacrificed herself daily. If there was chicken, she would take the leg; if there was a draught, she would sit in it—in short, she was so constituted that she would never have a mind or a wish of her own, but prefer to sympathize always with the minds and wishes of others."

Later, back in London, she kept posing questions: "Why did men drink wine and women water? Why was one sex so prosperous and the other so poor?" Wanting to "strain off what was personal and accidental in these impressions" of female subjugation, Woolf went to the British Library (which women had been allowed to enter for the previous two decades) and investigated the history of men's attitudes towards women down the ages. She found a stream of extraordinary prejudices and half-baked truths propounded with authority by priests, scientists and philosophers. Women were, it was said, ordained by God to be inferior; constitutionally unable to govern or run businesses; too weak to be doctors and, when they had their periods, incapable of handling machinery or remaining impartial during trial cases. Behind all this abuse, Woolf recognised, lay the problem of money. Women enjoyed no freedoms—including freedom of the spirit—because they did not control their own income: "Women have always been poor, not for two hundred years merely, but from the beginning of time. Women have had less intellectual freedom than the sons of Athenian slaves," she wrote.

Woolf's argument culminated in a set of specific political demands for women, including, at a minimum, dignity, equal rights to education, an income of "five hundred pounds a year" and "a room of one's own."

7.

The ideological element embedded within the modern status ideal may lack the shrill obnoxiousness of nineteenth-century pronouncements on race or gender—often it wears a smile and lies in innocuous places, within the bric-a-brac of what we read and hear—and yet it is equally partial and in certain situations equally prejudicial in its conception of what constitutes a good life. For this reason alone, it deserves greater scrutiny than it invites.

Society's ubiquitous statements and images convey messages to which we are less impervious than we like to admit. We must, for example, severely underestimate the subliminal powers of the Sunday newspaper if we trust that we may take in its contents and move on with our sense of priorities and desires no less altered than if we had spent the same two hours reading a chapter of Jacob Burckhardt's *The Civilisation of the Renaissance in Italy* or Saint Paul's Letter to the Galatians (the ritual of perusing the Sunday paper having, in the opinion of Max Weber, replaced that of attending church).

8.

What the political perspective seeks above all is an understanding of ideology. It aims to reach a point where ideology may be denaturalised and defused through analysis, enabling observers to exchange a puzzled, depressed response to it for a clear-eyed, genealogical grasp of its sources and effects.

When thoroughly investigated, the modern high-status ideal duly ceases to appear "natural" or God-given. It stands revealed instead as a development stemming from changes in industrial production and political organisation—changes that began in Britain in the second half of the eighteenth century and subsequently spread across the rest of Europe and North America. The enthusiasm for materialism, entrepreneurship and meritocracy that saturates the newspapers

The InterContinental London.
Ever heard of anyone dreaming of making it to the middle?
On the way to the top you can rarely mix business with pleasure. But that doesn't mean that the journey can't be pleasurable. We know what it takes.™
INTERCONTINENTAL
HOTELS & RESORTS
www.intercontinental.com 00 800 1800 1800

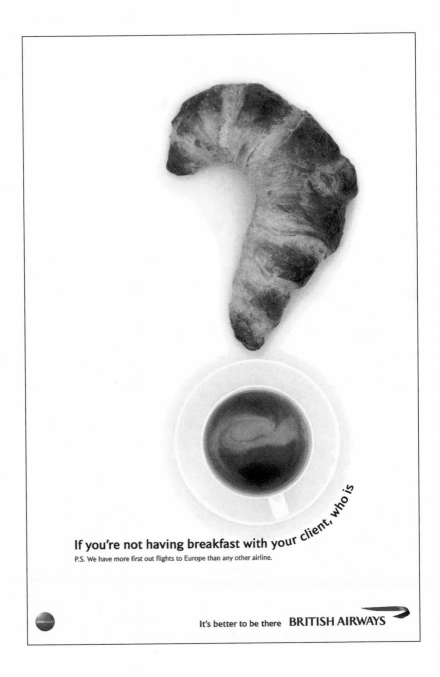

If you're not having breakfast with your client, who is

P.S. We have more first out flights to Europe than any other airline.

It's better to be there **BRITISH AIRWAYS**

and television schedules of our own day reflects nothing more complex than the interests of those in charge of the system by which the majority earn their living. "The ruling ideas of every age are always the ideas of the ruling class."

Unfortunately, understanding does not miraculously forestall any discomforts that may arise from the status ideal. Understanding bears the same relation to many of the difficulties of politics as a weather satellite to the crises of meteorology: it cannot always prevent problems, but it can at the very least teach us a host of useful things about the best ways to approach them, thereby sharply diminishing the sense of persecution, passivity and confusion we would otherwise feel. More ambitiously, understanding may also be a first step towards an attempt to shift, or tug at, a society's ideals, and thus to bring about a world in which it will be marginally less likely that veneration and honour will be dogmatically or unsceptically surrendered to those who are still wearing stilts.

IV
RELIGION

Death

1.

The hero of Tolstoy's novella *The Death of Ivan Ilyich* (1886) has long since fallen out of love with his wife. His children are a mystery to him, and he has no friends besides those who can advance his career or whose elevated positions will lend him some reflected glory. Ivan Ilyich is a man overwhelmingly concerned with status. He lives in Saint Petersburg, in a large apartment decorated according to the fashionable taste of the day, and gives frequent soulless dinner parties at which nothing warm or sincere is ever said. He works as a high court judge, a post he enjoys chiefly for the respect it brings him. Sometimes, late at night, Ivan Ilyich reads a book that is the "talk of the town," but only after he has discerned from magazines what line to take on it. Tolstoy sums up the judge's life in a single sentence: "The pleasures Ivan Ilyich derived from his work were those of pride; the pleasures he derived from society were those of vanity; but it was genuine pleasure that he derived from playing whist."

Then, at the age of forty-five, Ivan experiences a pain in his side that gradually spreads over his entire body. His doctors are at a loss to diagnose it: they talk vaguely and pretentiously of floating livers and inharmonious salt levels, and prescribe him a range of ever more expensive and ineffective medicines. Soon he is too tired to go to work; his intestines feel as if they were on fire; and he loses his appetite for food and, more significantly, for whist. It slowly dawns upon Ivan and all those around him that he will shortly be dead.

This is not, as it turns out, a wholly unwelcome prospect for many of Ivan's colleagues in the judiciary. Fyodor Vasilyevich predicts that with Ivan gone, he himself will probably get Shtabel's post, or Vinnikov's—a promotion worth an extra eight hundred rubles plus an allowance for office expenses. Another jurist, Pyotr Ivanovich, imagines that he will now be able to get his brother-in-law transferred from Kaluga, a move that will please his wife and ease tensions at home. The news is a little harder on the Ilyich family. Ivan's wife, while not directly regretting his imminent death, nevertheless worries about the size of her pension, while their socialite daughter fears that her father's funeral may play havoc with her wedding plans.

For his part, Ivan, with only a few weeks left to him, recognises that he has wasted his time on earth by leading an outwardly respectable but inwardly barren life. He scrolls back through his upbringing, education and career and finds that everything he has ever done has been motivated by the desire to appear important in the eyes of others, with his own interests and sensitivities always being sacrificed for the sake of impressing people who, he only now sees, do not care a jot for him. One night, as he lies awake in the early hours, racked by pain, "it occurred to him that those scarcely perceptible impulses of his to protest at what people of high status considered good, vague impulses which he had always suppressed, might have been precisely what mattered, and all the rest had not been the real thing. His official duties, his manner of life, his family, the values adhered to by people in society and in his profession—all these might not have been the real thing."

Ivan's regret at having squandered his brief life is compounded by the realisation that it is merely his status that those around him love, not his true, vulnerable self. He has won respect by being a judge, a wealthy father and a head of household, but with all of these assets about to be lost, in agony and afraid, he can no longer count on anyone's love: "What tormented Ivan Ilyich most was that no one gave him the kind of compassion he craved. There were moments after long suffering when what he wanted most of all (shameful as it might be for him to admit) was to be pitied like a sick child. He wanted to be caressed, kissed, cried over, as sick children are caressed and comforted. He knew that he was an important functionary with a greying beard, and so this was impossible; yet all the same he longed for it."

Once Ivan has breathed his last, his so-called friends come to pay their respects, though grumbling all the while at the disruption this obligation has caused in their card-playing schedule. The sight of his colleague's waxy, hollow face in the coffin is enough to make Pyotr Ivanovich consider that death may one day claim him, too—a fate that could have stern implications, especially for the logic that at present allows him to spend most of his time on whist: " 'Why, the same thing could happen to me at any time now,' thought Pyotr Ivanovich and for a moment he felt panic-stricken. But at once, he himself did not know how, he was rescued by the customary reflection that all this had happened to Ivan Ilyich, not to him, that it could not and should not happen to him; and that if he were to grant such a possibility, he would succumb to depression."

2.

The Death of Ivan Ilyich is, in the best tradition of the Christian memento mori, a study in how the idea of death may reorient our priorities away from the worldly and towards the spiritual, away from whist and dinner parties and towards truth and love.

Tolstoy's keen understanding of this phenomenon had its origins in personal experience: only a few years before writing *Ivan Ilyich*, he had questioned his own deepest concerns in the context of a new-found awareness of his mortality. In *A Confession* (1882), a record of that self-interrogation, he explained how at the age of fifty-one, with the publication of *War and Peace* and *Anna Karenina* behind him, world-famous and rich, he came to realise that he had long been living his life not by his own values, or even by God's, but by those of "society," which had inspired in him a restless desire to be stronger than others, more renowned, more important and richer. In his social circle, he noted, "ambition, love of power, covetousness, lasciviousness, pride, anger and revenge were all respected." But now, confronting the notion of death, he doubted the validity of his previous goals: " 'Well, you will have six thousand desyatinas of land in Samara Government and three hundred horses, and what then? . . . Very well; you will be more famous than Gogol or Pushkin or Shakespeare or Molière, or than all the writers in the world—and what of it?' I could find no reply at all."

The one answer that eventually silenced his questions was God: he resolved to spend the remainder of his days observing the teachings of Jesus Christ. Whatever we may make of the particularly Christian solution that Tolstoy adopted to his crisis of meaning, his sceptical journey follows a familiar trajectory. It is an example of how the thought of death may serve as a guide to a more genuine and more significant way of life. It is a solemn call, to follow Bach's Cantata BWV 106 (*Gottes Zeit ist die allerbeste Zeit*), to determine our true priorities:

Set thy house in order,	This is the ancient law:
For thou shalt die,	Man, thou must die.
And not remain alive.	Yea, come, Lord Jesus, come.
Bestelle dein Haus,	*Es ist der alte Bund:*
Denn du wirst Sterben,	*Mensch, du musst sterben.*
Und nicht lebendig bleiben.	*Ja, komm, Herr Jesus, Komm.*

3.

But how, specifically, might mortal illness help to orient us away from an excessive concern with status?

Principally, it may do so by relieving us of our capacity for many of the activities for which society honours its members, including throwing dinner parties, working effectively and dispensing patronage. Death thereby reveals the fragility, and so perhaps the worthlessness, of the attentions we stand to gain through status. In good health and at the height of our powers, we are spared any need to wonder whether those who pay us compliments are doing so out of sincere affection or in some evanescent quest for advantage. We seldom have the courage or the cynicism to ask, Is it *me* they're fond of, or *my position in society*? Illness, by felling the conditions of worldly love, renders the distinction quickly and all too cruelly evident. With death looming, clad in our hospital pyjamas, we are liable to turn in rage against our status-conditional lovers, as angry with ourselves for being vain enough to be seduced by them as we are with them for orchestrating their heartless seductions in the first place. The idea of death brings an authenticity to social life: there may be no better way to clear our calendar of engagements than to speculate as to who among our acquaintances would make the trip to our hospital bed.

As conditional love begins to lose its interest for us, so, too, may a number of the things we pursue in order to secure that love. If wealth, esteem and power buy us a kind of regard that will last only so long as our status holds, but conversely we are destined to end our lives defenceless and dishevelled, longing to be comforted like small children, then we have an unusually clear reason to concentrate our energies on those relationships which will best survive the erosion of our standing.

4.

Herodotus reported that it was the custom, towards the end of Egyptian feasts, when the revellers were at their most exuberant, for servants to march through the banqueting hall and among the tables carrying skeletons on stretchers. Regrettably, he did not go on to explain what effect this reminder of death was intended to have on the guests: would it make them keener to carry on with their merry-making, or send them home in a newfound mood of sobriety?

Typically, the thought of death may be expected, first, to usher us towards whatever happens to matter most to us (be it drinking beside the banks of the Nile, writing a book or making a fortune), and second, to encourage us to pay less attention to the verdicts of others—who will not, after all, be doing the dying for us. The prospect of our own extinction may draw us towards that way of life on which our hearts place the greatest value.

This theme animates "To His Coy Mistress" (1681), Andrew Marvell's famous poetic attempt to lure a hesitant young woman into bed, through lines that stress not only her beauty and his fidelity but also the less obviously romantic notion that both she and he will soon enough be stone dead. Addressing a subject who is apparently reluctant to express her desire due to anxiety over her reputation, Marvell uses the spectre of death to shift her attention away from her status within the community and towards her own wishes. He would not object to her coyness, he assures her, were it not for the fact that

> . . . at my back I always hear
> Time's wingèd chariot hurrying near;
> And yonder all before us lie
> Deserts of vast eternity. . . .
> The grave's a fine and private place,
> But none, I think, do there embrace.

Shakespeare, too, seemed eager to exploit death's amorous possibilities. One of his sonnets urges his beloved to anticipate the moment when

forty winters shall besiege thy brow
And dig deep trenches in thy beauty's field

even as another sonnet looks towards time's transformation of

your day of youth to sullied night

While the thought of death may occasionally be abused (to alarm individuals or groups into doing things they might never do otherwise), more often, and more hopefully, it may help us to correct our tendency to live as if we could afford to defer forever, for the sake of propriety, our underlying commitments to ourselves. Contemplating our mortality may give us the courage to unhook our lives from the more gratuitous of society's expectations. In the presence of a skeleton, the repressive aspects of others' opinions have a habit of shedding their power to intimidate.

5.

Whatever other differences there may be between them, Christian and secular concepts overlap substantially on the subject of what is meaningful in life when viewed from the perspective of death. There is a strikingly similar positive emphasis on love, authentic social relations and charity, and a common condemnation of the pursuit of power, military strength, wealth and glory. These and certain other ends and activities seem almost universally inconsequential beside the thought of death.

Elsewhere in his *Histories*, Herodotus tells us an apposite anecdote about Xerxes, the mighty king of Persia, who in 480 B.C. invaded Greece with an army of nearly two million men. Seeing the whole Hellespont filled with the vessels of his fleet, and the plains covered with his regiments, Xerxes at first congratulated himself on his good fortune and abilities. But then, a few moments later, he began to weep. His stunned uncle Artabanus, standing beside him, asked what a man in his position could possibly have to cry about. The king replied that he had just realised that in a hundred years' time, all these men arrayed before him, every one of the soldiers and sailors with whose help he had terrified the known world, would be dead.

We might feel no less sad, and no less sceptical about the value of fleeting achievements and impermanent notions of meaning, if we were to study a picture of the participants at a Heinz Company convention held in Chicago in the spring of 1902. The image of all these earnest men, each with his excited plan for increasing sales

Heinz salesmen, closing banquet, sales convention, Chicago, 1902

of ketchup and pickles in stores across the United States, should be enough to make us weep with the bitterness of King Xerxes of Persia.

Of course, the inevitable erasure of our earthly efforts at the hands of death is foreshadowed in other tasks besides conquering nations and building brands. We may observe a mother teaching her dimple-cheeked child to tie his shoelaces, and find ourselves haunted by an image of both of their eventual funerals. Nevertheless, we may conclude that bringing up a child is a more effective way of cheating death than selling condiments, or that helping a friend enjoys an advantage over leading an army.

"Vanity of Vanity, all is vanity," lamented the author of Ecclesiastes (1:2). "One generation passeth away, and another generation cometh; but the earth abideth for ever (1:4)." And yet it may be that, as Christian moralists would argue, not all things are equally vain. In some parts of Christendom, beginning in the sixteenth century, a new and very specific artistic genre emerged that would capture the imagination of the art-buying classes for the next two hundred years. Examples of "vanitas art," so named in tribute to Ecclesiastes, were hung in domestic environments, most often studies and bedrooms. Each still-life featured a table or sideboard on which was arranged a contrasting muddle of objects. There might be flowers, coins, a guitar or a mandolin, chess pieces, a book of verse, a laurel wreath or a wine bottle: symbols of frivolity and temporal glory. And somewhere among these would be set the two great symbols of death and the brevity of life: a skull and an hourglass.

The purpose of such works was not to send their viewers into a depression over the vanity of all things; rather, it was to embolden them to find fault with particular aspects of their own experience, while at the same time attending more closely to the virtues of love, goodness, sincerity, humility and kindness.

above: *Philippe de Champaigne,* Vanitas, *circa 1671*
opposite: *Simon Renard de Saint-André,* Vanitas, *circa 1662*

6.

If reflecting on our own mortality is instructive, we may also find some relief from status anxiety in dwelling on the deaths of other people—particularly those whose accomplishments in life have made us feel the most inadequate and envious. However forgotten and ignored we are, however powerful and revered others may be, we can take comfort in the thought that the lot of us will ultimately end up as that most democratic of substances: dust.

Outside the village of Walsingham, in Norfolk, in 1658, a farmer tilling his field felt his plough strike something odd. It turned out to be one in a row of fifty urns in which a group of aristocrats had been ceremoniously buried in either Roman or Saxon times. The discovery created a minor sensation in East Anglia, which soon enough came to the attention of a doctor living in Norwich. By the end of the year, Sir Thomas Browne, taking the long-buried urns as his starting point, had produced a digressive meditation on the futility of striving for worldly greatness, on human imperfectibility and on the related need to recognise our dependence on God for salvation. He entitled his essay "Urne-Buriall; or, A Brief Discourse of the Sepulchrall Urnes Lately Found in Norfolk."

"In a field of old Walsingham, not many moneths past, were digged up between fourty and fifty Urnes," reported Browne in his characteristic cadenced, lumpy English, "deposited in a dry and sandy soile, not a yard deep, nor farre from one another . . . some containing two pounds of bones, distinguishable in skulls, ribs, jawes, thigh-bones and teeth." What interested Browne was how the identities of the dead, in their day the wealthiest and most important people in the area, had been entirely lost to history. Some had theorised that the remains were those of Romans, for the burial site was not far from an old Roman garrison; Browne, however, conjectured that they were more likely to be "our Brittish, Saxon or Danish Forefathers." In any case, no one would ever know their names, let alone in what century they had lived and died. From this, Browne moved on to reflect on the power of time to make a mockery of all human claims to earthly achievement and distinction: "Who knows the fate of his bones, or how often he is to be buried?" he asked, challenging the dead aristocrats, who must once have felt confident of their place in the world, and hosted receptions and played the lyre and looked proudly at themselves in the mirror in the morning. "There is no antidote against the opium of time," Browne admonished. "Generations passe while some trees stand, and old Families last not three Oaks." Rather than try to achieve fame on earth, the duty of the honest Christian was to make an impression "not in the record of man" but instead "in the Register of God."

The message may seem a melancholy one, but it is arguably much more so for those who anchor their lives on the pleasures of a high-status position than it is for those whom society ignores and who are therefore already well acquainted with the oblivion in which their privileged counterparts will someday join them. It is the rich, the beautiful, the famous and the powerful for whom death has in store the cruellest lessons—the very categories of people, that is, whose worldly goods take them, in the Christian understanding, furthest from God.

In England, in the middle of the eighteenth century, this Christian-inspired moral was given repeated expression by a group of poets known as the Graveyard School. The name referred to their specialty: poems in which the narrator finds himself in a churchyard on a starry, moonlit night and, beside some semidefaced graves, begins musing on the power of death to wipe away success and glory (a phenomenon that clearly did not distress the poets overmuch but seemed indeed to be a source of barely suppressed joy). In Edward Young's poem "Night Thoughts" (1742), for instance, the speaker, sitting on a moss-covered gravestone, lets his mind turn to the shared fate of all the great men of the past:

> The sage, peer, potentate, king, conqueror
> Death humbles these.
> Why all this toil for triumphs of an hour?
> What though we wade in wealth, or soar in fame,
> Earth's highest station ends in "Here he lies":
> And "Dust to dust" concludes her noblest song.

Young's contemporary, Robert Blair, in "The Grave" (1743), set in another churchyard, picked up on the same theme:

> When self-esteem, or others' adulation,
> Would cunningly persuade us we are something
> Above the common level of our kind
> The grave gainsays the smooth-complexioned flattery
> And with blunt truth acquaints us with what we are.

The message was reiterated by the most distinguished poet of the Graveyard School, Thomas Gray, in his "Elegy Written in a Country Churchyard" (1751):

> The boast of heraldry, the pomp of power,
> And all that beauty, all that wealth ever gave,
> Awaits alike the inevitable hour.
> The paths of glory lead but to the grave.

For those treated roughly by society, there is some sweet, preemptive revenge to be had in anticipating the eventual demise of certain of its members.

A number of artists have similarly delighted in depicting their

Hubert Robert, Imaginary View of the Grande Gallerie of the Louvre in Ruins, *1796*

Joseph Gandy, View of the Rotunda of the Bank of England in Ruins, *1798*

own civilisation in a tattered future form, as a warning to, and reprisal against, the pompous guardians of the age. So fond was one such, the eighteenth-century painter Hubert Robert, of painting the great buildings of modern France in ruins that he earned himself the sobriquet Robert des Ruines. Across the Channel, meanwhile, Robert's contemporary Joseph Gandy would make a name for himself by portraying the Bank of England with its ceiling caved in.

Some seventy years later, Gustave Doré was to illustrate London as he fancied it would look in the twenty-first century. His latter-day version of ancient Rome is complete with a caped figure—identified in the work's title as a New Zealander, an inhabitant of the country that in Doré's day symbolised the future—sketching the ruins of the then-brand-new Cannon Street Station, much as Grand Touring Englishmen had once gone to Athens or Rome to sketch the Parthenon or the Colosseum.

From the eighteenth century onwards, inspired by like sentiments, European travellers set out on journeys to contemplate ruins of the past: Troy, Corinth, Paestum, Thebes, Mycenae, Knossos, Palmyra, Baalbec, Petra and Pompeii. The Germans, masters that they were at formulating compound names for fugitive and rare states of the soul (*Weltschmerz, Schadenfreude, Wanderlust,* to cite just a few), coined terms to describe the new feeling for old stones: *Ruinenempfindsamkeit, Ruinensehnsucht, Ruinenlust.* In March 1787, Goethe twice visited Pompeii. "Many a calamity has happened in the world," he wrote from Naples, "but never one that has caused so much entertainment to posterity as this one." "What wonderful mornings I have spent in the Colosseum, lost in some corner of those vast ruins!" remembered Stendhal in his *Promenades dans Rome* (1829). After recommending ruin-gazing as "the most intense

Gustave Doré, The New Zealander, 1871

Above: *David Roberts*, General View of Baalbec, *1842*
Left: *David Roberts*, Doorway at Baalbec, *1842*

pleasure that memory can procure," he went so far as to declare that the Colosseum was more attractive in its present, crumbling state than it ever could have been when newly built.

"My name is Ozymandias, king of kings: / Look on my works, ye mighty, and despair!" reads an inscription on the pedestal of a statue of Ramses II of Egypt, according to Shelley's "Ozymandias" (1818). But there is no need for the mighty, or even the humble, to obey the second command, for the Pharaoh himself lies in pieces on the ground, and "round the decay / Of that colossal wreck, boundless and bare / The lone and level sands stretch far away."

237

Ruins reprove us for our folly in sacrificing peace of mind for the unstable rewards of earthly power. Beholding old stones, we may feel our anxieties over our achievements—and the lack of them—slacken. What does it matter, really, if we have not succeeded in the eyes of others, if there are no monuments and processions in our honour or if no one smiled at us at a recent gathering? Everything is, in any event, fated to disappear, leaving only New Zealanders to sketch the ruins of our boulevards and offices. Judged against eternity, how little of what agitates us makes any difference.

Ruins bid us to surrender our strivings and our fantasies of perfection and fulfilment. They remind us that we cannot defy time and that we are merely the playthings of forces of destruction which can at best be kept at bay but never vanquished. We may enjoy local victories, perhaps claim a few years in which we are able to impose a degree of order upon the chaos, but ultimately all will slop back into a primeval soup. If this prospect has the power to console us, it is perhaps because the greater part of our anxieties stems from an exaggerated sense of the importance of our own projects and concerns. We are tortured by our ideals and by a punishingly high-minded sense of the gravity of what we are doing.

Christian moralists have long understood that to the end of reassuring the anxious, they will do well to emphasise that contrary to the first principle of optimism, everything will in fact turn out for the *worst:* the ceiling will collapse, the statue will topple, we will die, everyone we love will vanish and all our achievements and even our names will be trod underfoot. We may derive some comfort from this, however, if a part of us is able instinctively to recognise how closely our miseries are bound up with the grandiosity of our ambitions. To consider our petty status worries from the perspective of a thousand years hence is to be granted a rare, tranquillising glimpse of our own insignificance.

7.

Vast landscapes can have much the same anxiety-reducing effect on us as ruins, for they are the representatives of infinite space, as ruins are the representatives of infinite time. Against them, or within them, our weak, short-lived bodies must seem of no greater consequence than those of moths or spiders.

Then, too, whatever differences exist among people, they are as nothing next to the differences between the most powerful humans and the great deserts, high mountains, glaciers and oceans of the world. There are natural phenomena so enormous as to make the variations between any two people seem mockingly tiny. By seeking these out, and experiencing a consoling sense of the insignificance of all humans within the cosmos, we may mitigate whatever discomfort we feel over our inferior position in the social hierarchy.

In sum, we may best overcome a feeling of unimportance not by making ourselves more important but by recognising the relative lack of importance of everyone on earth. Our concern with who is a few millimetres taller than us (*above right*) may thus give way to an awe for things a thousand million times larger than any human being (*right*), a force that we may be moved to call infinity, eternity—or simply, and perhaps most usefully, God.

8.

A fine remedy for our anxieties over our low status in society may be to travel—whether literally or figuratively, by viewing works of art—through the gigantic spaces of the world.

Frederic Edwin Church, Niagara, 1857

Thomas Moran, Nearing Camp, Evening on the Upper Colorado River, Wyoming, *1882*

Albert Bierstadt, Western Landscape, *1869*

Community

1.

According to one influential wing of modern secular society, there are few more disreputable fates than to end up being "like everyone else"—for "everyone else" is a category that embraces the mediocre and the conformist, the boring and the suburban. The goal of all right-thinking people, so this argument goes, should be to distinguish themselves from the crowd and "stand out" in whatever way their talents will allow.

2.

But being like everyone else is not, if we follow Christian thought, any kind of calamity, for it was one of Jesus' central claims that all human beings, including the slow-witted, the untalented and the obscure, were beloved creatures of God—and hence deserving of the honour owed to every example of his work. In the words of Saint Peter, each of us has the capacity to be a partaker "of the divine nature," an idea that in and of itself audaciously challenges the assumption that some are born to mediocrity and others to glory. No one is outside the circle of God's love, Christianity insists, attributing divine authority to the notion of mutual respect. What we have in common with others comprises what is most cherishable in ourselves.

Christianity bids us to look beyond our superficial differences in order to focus on what it considers to be a set of universal truths, on which a sense of community and kinship may be built. Whether we are cruel or impatient, dim or dull, we must recognise that we are all of us detained and bound together by shared vulnerabilities.

Beneath our flaws, there are always two driving forces: fear and the desire for love.

To encourage fellow feeling, Jesus urged his followers to learn to look at other adults as they might at children. Few things can more quickly transform our sense of a person's character than picturing him or her as a child; from this perspective, we are better able to express the sympathy and generosity that we all but naturally display towards the young, whom we tend to describe as naughty rather than bad, cheeky rather than arrogant. This is the same sort of softening we may feel towards anyone whom we see sleeping: with eyes closed and features relaxed and defenceless, a sleeper invites a gentle regard that in itself is almost love—so much so, in fact, that it can be unsettling to gaze at length at a stranger asleep beside us on a train or plane. That unmasked face seems to prompt us towards an intimacy that calls into question the foundations of civilised indifference on which ordinary communal relations rest. But there is no such thing as a stranger, a Christian would say; there is only the *impression* of strangeness, born out of a failure to acknowledge that others share both our needs and our weaknesses. Nothing could be nobler, or more fully human, than to perceive that we are indeed fundamentally, in every way that really matters, just like everyone else.

3.

The idea that other people might be at base neither incomprehensible nor distasteful carries weighty implications for our concern with status, given that the desire to achieve social distinction is to a great extent fuelled by a horror of being—or even being *thought*—"ordinary." The more humiliating, shallow, debased or ugly we take ordinariness to be, the stronger will be our desire to set ourselves apart. The more corrupt the community, the stronger the lure of individual achievement.

Since its beginnings, Christianity has attempted to enhance, both in practical and in theoretical terms, the value its adherents place on belonging to a community. One notable way it has achieved this is through the repetition of rituals, from the saying of the service to prayer to the singing of hymns—each an opportunity for a large number of unrelated celebrants to feel their suspicion of one another abate thanks to a transcendent intermediary.

Music in any form can be a great leveller. We might, for example, imagine joining an unfamiliar congregation within the walls of a cathedral to hear Bach's *Mass in B Minor* ("the greatest work of music of all ages and of all peoples," in the view of Hans-Georg Nägeli, writing in 1817). Much may separate us: age, income, clothes and background. We may never before have spoken to one another and may be wary of letting anyone catch our gaze. But as the *Mass* begins, so, too, does a process of social alchemy. The music conveys feelings that had hitherto seemed inchoate and private, and our eyes may fill with tears of relief and gratitude for the gift given us by the composer and musicians in making audible, and hence available to us and to others, the movements of our collective soul. Violins, voices, flutes, double basses, oboes, bassoons and trumpets combine to create sounds that evoke the most secret, most elusive aspects of our psyches. Moreover, the public nature of the performance helps us to realise that if others around us are responding as we are to the music, then they cannot be the indecipherable enigmas we imagined them to be. Their emotions run along the same tracks as ours, they are stirred by the very same things and so, whatever the differences in our appearance and manner, we possess a common core, out of which a connection can be forged and extended far beyond this one occasion. A group of strangers who initially seemed so foreign may thus in time, through the power of choral music, acquire some of the genuine intimacy of friends, slipping out from behind their stony facades to share, if only briefly, in a beguiling vision of humankind.

4.

But of course, our sense of who other people are is seldom so flattering outside the cathedral. The public arena is usually more decrepit and threatening, sending us scurrying in search of physical and psychological cover.

There are countries in which the communal provision of housing, transport, education and health care is so inferior that inhabitants will naturally seek to escape involvement with the masses by barricading themselves behind solid walls. The desire for high status is never stronger than in situations where "ordinary" life fails to answer a median need for dignity and comfort.

Then there are communities—far fewer in number and typically imbued with a strong (often Protestant) Christian heritage—whose public realms exude respect in their principles and architecture, and whose citizens are therefore under less compulsion to retreat into a private domain. Indeed, we may find that some of our ambitions for personal glory fade when the public spaces and facilities to which we enjoy access are themselves glorious to behold; in such context, ordinary citizenship may come to seem an adequate goal. In Switzerland's largest city, for instance, the need to own a car in order to avoid sharing a bus or train with strangers loses some of the urgency it has in Los Angeles or London, thanks to Zurich's superlative tram network, which is clean, safe, warm and edifying in its punctuality and technical prowess. There is little reason to travel in an automotive cocoon when, for a fare of only a few francs, an efficient, stately tramway will provide transportation from point A to point B at a level of comfort an emperor might have envied.

One insight to be drawn from Christianity and applied to communal ethics is that, insofar as we can recover a sense of the preciousness of every human being and, even more important, legislate for spaces and manners that embody such a reverence in their makeup, then the notion of the ordinary will shed its darker associations, and, correspondingly, the desires to triumph and to be insulated will weaken, to the psychological benefit of all.

In an ideal Christian community, the dread of "losers" having to live alongside the "winners" will be tempered and contained by a basic equality of dignity and resources. And the dichotomy between succeeding/flourishing and failing/withering will lose some of its excruciating sharpness.

Twin Cities

1.

One of Christianity's central themes may be traced back to Jesus' choice of career. The carpenters of Galilee practised a semiskilled but insecure and rarely lucrative trade, and yet Jesus was all the same, in Saint Peter's phrase, "the right hand of Heaven," the son of God, the king of kings, sent to save us from our sins. That someone could combine within himself two such different identities, being at once an itinerant tradesman and the holiest of men, forms the basis upon which the Christian understanding of status is built. Every person possesses, in this framework, two wholly unrelated types of status: the earthly kind, determined by occupation, income and the opinions of others; and the spiritual sort, meted out according to the quality of the individual's soul and his or her merit in the eyes of God after the Day of Judgement. One might therefore be powerful and revered in the earthly realm, yet barren and corrupt in the spiritual one. Or one might be like the beggar Lazarus in the Gospel of Saint Luke, who had only rags to his name while glorying in divine riches.

In *The City of God* (A.D. 427), Saint Augustine explained that all human actions could be interpreted from either a Christian or a Roman perspective, and that the very accomplishments that were esteemed most highly by the Romans—amassing money, building villas, winning wars and so on—counted for nothing in the Christian schema, in which a new set of concerns, including loving one's neighbours, being humble and generous and recognising one's dependence on God, offered the keys to elevated status. Augustine's figure for these two value systems was a pair of cities, the City of God and the Earthly City, which he described as being, until the Day of

Judgement, coexistent but separate. One might thus be a king in the Earthly City but a mere manservant in the heavenly one.

Nine centuries later, Dante would flesh out Augustine's ideas by providing a detailed accounting of who would end up where in that ultimate twinned embodiment of the Christian hierarchy: Heaven and Hell. In the *Divine Comedy* (1315), he enumerated no fewer than nine different circles of Hell (with seventeen distinct rings), each one reserved for a particular kind of sin; and set opposite those, ten spheres of Heaven, each the province of a specific virtue. The religious hierarchy resembled a distorted or inverted version of its secular counterpart. Dante's Hell was home to a wide range of individuals who had enjoyed high status during their life on earth: generals, writers, poets, emperors, bishops, popes and merchants, all now stripped of their privileges and enduring extreme sufferings as punishment for having offended God's laws. In the fourth ring of the ninth circle of Hell, Dante (touring the place with Virgil) hears the screams of those who were powerful but treacherous when alive, now being chewed in the mouths of the three-headed giant Lucifer. In the first ring of the seventh circle, the poet finds himself by a river of boiling blood in which Alexander the Great and Attila the Hun struggle to stay afloat while, from the riverbank, a group of centaurs fire arrows over their heads to force them back under the sickening froth. In the fifth circle, an array of angry, prominent leaders whose tempers once cost the lives of others languish in a swampy, fetid cesspool, choking on mud; and in the third circle, excrement rains down upon those who used to be gluttonous.

The liturgical discrepancy between heavenly and earthly status promised believers a way out of an oppressive, one-dimensional vision of success. Christianity did not do away altogether with the concept of a hierarchy; its contribution was, rather, to redefine success and failure in ethical, nonmaterial terms, by insisting that

Gustave Doré, The Violent Tortured in the Rain of Fire, *1861*

Gustave Doré, The Thieves Tortured by Serpents, *1861*

poverty could coexist with goodness, and a humble occupation with a noble soul: "A man's life consisteth not in the abundance of the things which he possesseth," according to Saint Luke, a follower of that impecunious carpenter from Galilee.

2.

But far from merely asserting the superiority of spiritual over material success, Christianity also endowed the values it revered with a seductive seriousness and beauty, accomplishing this in part through the magisterial use of painting, literature, music and architecture. It employed works of art to make a case for virtues that had never before figured prominently—if at all—in the priorities of rulers or their subjects.

For hundreds of years, the talents of the finest stonemasons, poets, musicians and painters—whose predecessors had been called upon to celebrate the triumphs of emperors and the blood-curdling victories of legions over barbarian hordes—were directed towards praising such activities as giving alms and showing respect for the poor. The glorification of worldly values never entirely disappeared in the Christian era—there remained plenty of palaces to alert the world to the charms of mercantile or landed wealth and power—but for a time, in many communities, the most impressive buildings on the horizon were those that honoured the nobility of poverty rather than the might of a royal family or corporation, and the most moving pieces of music sang not of personal fulfilment but of the torment of the Son of God, who had been, in the words of Isaiah 53:3, quoted in Handel's *Messiah* (1741),

despised and rejected of men;
a man of sorrows, and acquainted with grief

Through its command of aesthetic resources, of buildings, paintings and Masses, Christianity created a bulwark against the authority of earthly values and kept its spiritual concerns in the public eye and at the forefront of the public mind.

In the four centuries between approximately 1130 and 1530, in towns and cities all over Europe, more than a hundred cathedrals were erected, their spires coming to dominate the skyscape, looming above grain stores, palaces, offices, factories and homes. Possessed of a grandeur that few other structures could rival, they offered a venue in which people from every walk of life could gather to ponder ideas that were, at least in the context of the history of architecture, highly unusual: ideas about the value of sadness and innocence, of meekness and pity. Whereas a city's other buildings were designed to serve earthly needs—housing and feeding the body, allowing it to rest, manufacturing machines and implements to assist it—the cathedral had as its unique functions to empty the mind of egoistic projects and lead it towards God and his love. City dwellers engaged in worldly tasks could, during the course of a day, on seeing the outlines of these great massings of stone, be reminded of a vision of life that challenged the authority of ordinary ambitions. A cathedral such as Chartres, whose spires soar 107 metres into the sky (the height of a thirty-four-storey skyscraper), was understood to be the home of the dispossessed, a symbol of the rewards they would reap in the next life. However ramshackle their present physical dwellings, the cathedral was where they belonged in their heart. Its beauties reflected their inner worth, as its stained glass windows and coffered ceilings made vivid the glory of Jesus' message to them.

3.

Christianity did not, of course, ever succeed in abolishing the Earthly City or its values, and yet if we retain some distinction

between wealth and virtue and still ask of people whether they are good rather than merely important, it is in large part due to the impression left upon Western consciousness by a religion that for centuries lent its resources and prestige to the defence of a handful of

extraordinary ideas regarding the rightful distribution of status. It was the genius of the artists and craftsmen who worked in the service of Christianity to give enduring form to its ideals and to make these real to us through their handling of stone, glass, sound, word and image.

In a world where secular buildings whisper to us relentlessly of the importance of earthly power, the cathedrals that punctuate the skylines of great towns and cities may continue to furnish an imaginative holding space for the priorities of the spirit.

V
BOHEMIA

Lee Miller, Le Déjeuner sur L'Herbe, *1937. A group of Surrealist friends on a picnic in Mougins, France: on the left, Nusch and Paul Eluard; on the right, from top, Roland Penrose, Man Ray and Ady Fidelin.*

1.

At the beginning of the nineteenth century, a new group of people started to attract notice in western Europe and the United States. They often dressed simply; they lived in the cheaper parts of town; they read a lot; they seemed not to care much about money; they were frequently of melancholic temperament; their allegiances were to art and emotion rather than to business and material success; they sometimes had unconventional sexual lives and some of the women wore their hair short before it was the fashion. They came to be collectively described as "bohemian." Traditionally used to refer to Gypsies (because they were mistakenly thought to have originated in central Europe), the word evolved—especially following the success of *Scènes de la vie de Bohême* (1851), Henri Murger's account of life in the garrets and cafés of Paris—to encompass a wider range of people who did not, for one reason or another, fit into the bourgeois conception of respectability.

From the outset, bohemia was a democratic church. Early reporters suggested that bohemians could be found in every social class, age group and profession: they were men and women, rich and poor, poets and lawyers, scientists and the unemployed. Arthur Ransome, in *Bohemia in London* (1907), observed, "Bohemia can be anywhere: it is not a place but an attitude of mind." There have been bohemian enclaves in Cambridge, Massachusetts, and Venice Beach, California; bohemians living in grand houses with servants and in huts on the shores of quiet lakes; outwardly conventional bohemians and ones with a taste for bathing naked by moonlight. One can wind the label around a number of different artistic and social phenomena of the last two hundred years, from romanticism to surrealism, from the Beatniks to the Punks, from the Situationists to the Kibbutzniks, and still not break a thread that binds together something important.

In London in 1929, the bohemian poet Brian Howard invited his

friends to a party. The invitation card bore a list of his likes and dis-
likes—which, for all their peculiarly early-twentieth-century En-
glishness, impart some flavour of the characteristic inclinations and
fears that bohemians have manifested throughout their history.

What Brian Howard and his fellow bohemians disliked might
more succinctly have been summed up in a single term: "the bourgeoisie." Having come to prominence during the same historical
period—in France, after the fall of Napoleon, in 1815—bohemians

J'Accuse	J'Adore
Ladies and Gentlemen	Men and Women
Public Schools	Nietzsche
Debutantes	Picasso
Sadist devotees of blood-sports	Kokoschka
"Eligible bachelors"	Jazz
Missionaries	Acrobats
People who worry they can't meet so-and-so because they've got "a bad reputation"	The Mediterranean D. H. Lawrence Havelock Ellis
The young men one meets at boring parties in stuck-up moronic country houses	The sort of people who know they haven't got immortal souls; and are not anticipating—after death—any rubbishy reunion, apotheosis or ANYTHING

nursed a ferocious disdain for almost everything the bourgeois stood for, and took particular pride in heaping extravagant insults on them.

"Hatred of the bourgeois is the beginning of wisdom," wrote Gustave Flaubert. It was a standard utterance for any self-respecting mid-nineteenth-century French writer, such contempt being as much a matter of professional honour as having an affair with an actress or taking a trip to the Orient. Flaubert accused the bourgeois of extreme prudery and materialism, of being at once cynical and sentimental, of immersing themselves in trivia—so that they might spend an age, for example, debating whether melon was a vegetable or a fruit and whether it should be eaten as a starter (in the French manner) or a dessert (the English way). Stendhal, no fonder of this class, complained, "The conversation of the true bourgeois about men and life, which is no more than a collection of ugly details, brings on a profound attack of spleen when I am obliged to listen to it for any length of time."

What ultimately separated bohemia from the bourgeoisie, however, was not the choice of conversational topics or desserts, but the answer to the questions of who deserved high status and why. From the outset, real bohemians were those who, whether they owned a mansion or squatted in a garret, set themselves up as saboteurs of the economic meritocracy to which the early nineteenth century gave birth.

2.

At the heart of the conflict lay a contrasting assessment of the value of worldly achievement, on the one hand, and sensitivity, on the other. Whereas the bourgeoisie accorded status on the basis of commercial success and public reputation, for bohemians what mattered above all else, and certainly above the ability to pay for an elegant home or chic clothes, was openness to the wider world and devotion, whether on the creative or the appreciative end, to the primary repository of feeling that was art. The martyrs of the bohemian value system were those who sacrificed the security of a regular job and the esteem of society for the opportunity to write, paint or make music, to dedicate themselves to travel or to spend time with their friends and families. They might, because of their commitments, lack the accoutrements, and perhaps even the manners, of outward decency, yet they were still, the bohemians themselves averred, deserving of the highest honour for their ethical good sense and their powers of receptivity and expression.

Many bohemians were prepared to suffer or even starve for their impractical beliefs. Nineteenth-century portraits often depicted them slouched on chairs in the dirty attic rooms of apartment blocks, their countenance gaunt and exhausted. There might be a faraway glint in their eyes and a skull on their bookshelves, and the look on their face might be such as to frighten a factory fore-man or office manager—a sign that the bohemian soul was not taken up by the shallow, utilitarian concerns that so obsessed the bourgeoisie.

Such destitution was, for a bohemian, vastly to be preferred to the horror of wasting his life on a job he despised. Charles Baudelaire declared that all occupations were soul-destroying, save for writing poetry and—even less plausibly—being a "warrior." When Marcel Duchamp visited New York in 1915, he described Greenwich Village as a "true Bohemia" because the place was, he said, "full of people doing *nothing*." Half a century later, Jack Kerouac, addressing an audience in a West Coast piano bar, would rail against "the com-muters with their tight collars obliged to catch the 5:48 a.m. train at Millbrae or San Carlos to get to work in San Francisco," and praise in their stead the free spirits, bums, poets, beats and artists who slept

Formerly attributed to Théodore Géricault, now unknown,
Portrait of an Artist in His Studio, *circa 1820*

Gustave Courbet, Portrait of the Artist (Man with a Pipe), *circa 1848–1849*

late and burned their work clothes so as to become "sons of the road and watch the freight trains pass, take in the immensity of the sky and feel the weight of ancestral America."

If bohemians did not argue that there was any *theoretical* incompatibility between having an intense life of the mind and owning a profitable law firm or factory, most implied that there might be a *practical* conflict. In the preface to *On Love* (1822), Stendhal explained that while he had attempted to write clearly and for a broad audience, he could not supply "hearing to the deaf nor sight to the blind." "So people with money and coarse pursuits, who have made a 100,000 francs in the year before they open this book, had better close it again quickly, particularly if they are bankers, manufacturers, or respectable industrialists . . . The active, hardworking, eminently respectable and positive life of a privy councillor, a textile manufacturer or a clever banker reaps its reward in wealth but not in tender sensations. Little by little the hearts of these gentlemen ossify. People who pay 2,000 workmen at the end of every week do not *waste their time* like this; their minds are always bent on useful and positive things." Stendhal felt his book would be best appreciated by that rare reader who had a taste for indolence, liked daydreaming, welcomed the emotions sparked by a performance of one of Mozart's operas and could be catapulted into hours of bittersweet musing after catching just one glimpse of a beautiful face in a crowded street.

The idea that money and workaday occupations must corrupt the soul—or destroy the capacity for, in Stendhal's words, "tender sensations"—has reverberated down the history of bohemia. It can, for example, be heard no less clearly, nearly a century and a half after Stendhal's lament, in Charles Bukowski's poem "Something for the Touts, the Nuns, the Grocery Clerks and You" (1965), which evokes the lives of wealthy businessmen:

with bad breath and big feet, men
who look like frogs, hyenas, men who walk
as if melody had never been invented, men
who think it is intelligent to hire and fire and
profit, men with expensive wives they possess
like sixty acres of ground to be drilled
or shown-off or to be walled away from
the incompetent . . .
. . . men who stand in front of
windows thirty feet wide and see nothing,
men with luxury yachts who can sail around
the world and yet never get out of their vest
pockets, men like snails, men like eels, men
like slugs, and not as good.

Just as money cannot purchase honour within the bohemian value system, neither can possessions command it: seen through bohemian eyes, yachts and mansions are merely symbols of arrogance and frivolity. Bohemian status is more likely to be earned through an inspired conversational style or authorship of an intelligent, heartfelt volume of verse.

In July 1845, Henry Thoreau, one of the most renowned bohemians of nineteenth-century America, moved into a cabin he had built with his own hands on the northern shore of Walden Pond, near the town of Concord, Massachusetts. It was his ambition to embark on an outwardly simple but inwardly rich existence, and in the process demonstrate to the bourgeoisie that it was possible to combine a life of material scarcity with one of psychological fulfilment. Proving just how inexpensive subsistence could be once one ceased to worry about impressing others, Thoreau provided a breakdown of the minimal costs he had incurred in building his new home:

Boards.	$8.03 ¹/₂ (mostly shanty boards)
Refuse shingles for roof and sides	4.00
Laths	1.25
Two second-hand windows with glass	2.43
One thousand old bricks	4.00
Two casks of lime.	2.40 (That was high.)
Hair.	0.31 (More than I needed.)
Mantle-tree iron	0.15
Nails	3.90
Hinges and screws.	0.14
Latch.	0.10
Chalk.	0.01
Transportation.	1.40 (I carried a good part on my back.)
In all	$28.12 ¹/₂

"Most of the luxuries, and many of the so-called comforts of life, are not only not indispensable, but positive hindrances to the elevation of mankind," wrote Thoreau. Then, in a bid to break, or upend, society's link between owning things and being honourable, he added, "Man is rich in proportion to the number of things he can do without."

With *Walden,* Thoreau tried to reconfigure our sense of what a lack of means might indicate about a person. It was not, as the bourgeois perspective tended more or less subtly to suggest, always a sign that one was a loser at the game of life; instead, it might simply signify that one had opted to focus one's energies on activities other than making money, thereby enriching one's life in other ways. Dissatisfied with the word *poverty* as a descriptor for his own condition, Thoreau preferred *simplicity,* which he felt conveyed a consciously

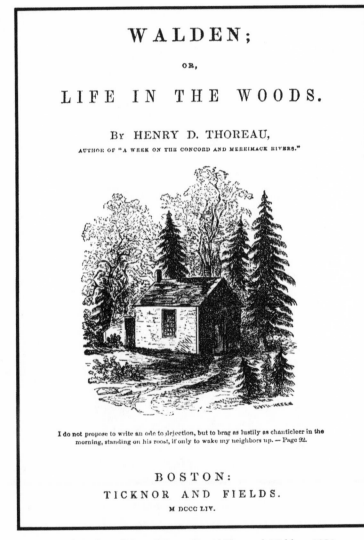

WALDEN;

OR,

LIFE IN THE WOODS.

By HENRY D. THOREAU,

AUTHOR OF "A WEEK ON THE CONCORD AND MERRIMACK RIVERS."

I do not propose to write an ode to dejection, but to brag as lustily as chanticleer in the morning, standing on his roost, if only to wake my neighbors up. — Page 92.

BOSTON:
TICKNOR AND FIELDS.
M DCCC LIV.

Title page of the first edition of Henry David Thoreau's Walden, *1854* chosen, rather than an imposed, material situation. After all, he reminded the merchants of Boston, people no less noble than the "Chinese, Hindoo, Persian and Greek philosophers" had once pursued, of their own accord, a simple way of life. The tenor of the message that Thoreau took away from his stay on the shores of Walden Pond, and later delivered to the burgeoning industrialised society of the United States, would have been familiar to almost every bohemian who came before and after him. As he put it, "Money is not required to buy one necessary of the soul."

3.

One acute insight that may be attributed to bohemia is that one's ability to maintain confidence in a way of life at odds with the mainstream culture will be greatly dependent on the operative value system of one's immediate environment, on the kinds of people one mixes with socially and on what one reads and listens to.

Most bohemians recognise that their peace of mind may be only too easily shattered, and their commitments brazenly challenged, by conversing for a few minutes with an acquaintance who feels, even if he or she does not say so explicitly, that money and a public profile are ultimately estimable. The same disruption may result from reading a newspaper or magazine that, by reporting exclusively on the feats of bourgeois success stories, insidiously undermines the worth of any alternative ambitions.

Bohemians in consequence tend to take particular care in choosing their companions. Some attempt, like Thoreau, to escape the corrupting influence of society altogether. Others assiduously create communities of congenial spirits, refusing to indulge in the kind of socialising that the rest of us so readily fall into with whoever happens to be on hand—usually an assortment of characters with whom we are thrown together at school, in our families or at work.

The photographer Lee Miller and her friend the model Tanja Ramm, in Miller's studio in Montparnasse, Paris, 1931

In the world's large cities, bohemians are apt to cluster in the same districts to ensure that their daily contacts will be with genuine friends rather than with status-concerned acquaintances. The history of bohemia is punctuated by the names of places rendered famous by the friendships formed there: Montparnasse, Bloomsbury, Chelsea, Greenwich Village, Venice Beach.

4.

Bohemia has also carefully redefined its understanding of the word *failure.*

In the bourgeois lexicon, any financial or critical failure in business or the arts rises to the level of a significant indictment of an individual's character, given the bourgeoisie's ideological assumption that society is essentially fair in distributing its rewards. Bohemians, however, refute this punitive interpretation of outward failure by pointing out how often the world is governed by idiocy and prejudice. Human nature being what it is, they reason, those who succeed in society will rarely be the wisest or the best; rather, they will be the ones who are able to pander most effectively to the flawed values of their audiences. There may indeed, bohemians hint, be no more damning marker of a person's ethical and imaginative limitations than a capacity for commercial success.

Such a perspective explains the interest and respect accorded by many nineteenth-century bohemians to political, artistic and literary figures whose lives could only have been described as failures according to the bourgeois scale of values. The most celebrated of these was the minor English poet Thomas Chatterton, who committed suicide in 1770, at the age of eighteen, worn down by poverty and the rejection of his work by his patrons. Alfred de Vigny's play *Chatterton,* first performed in Paris in 1835, turned the young poet into a mouthpiece for all the values that bohemia held dear. The play

Henry Wallis, The Death of Chatterton, *1855–1856*

championed personal inspiration over tradition, kindness over financial advantage, intensity and madness over rationality and utilitarianism. De Vigny's message was that talented, delicate men of letters were all but fated to be driven to despair and even suicide by the crass tastes of their bourgeois public.

The myth of the misunderstood artist—the outsider who is nevertheless, despite critical failure, superior to the insider—reflected or shaped the lives of many of the greatest heroes of bohemia. Gérard de Nerval, a poet more talented than Chatterton but no happier, hanged himself in 1855, destitute and mad at forty-seven. Summing up the history of his generation of sensitive brethren, whose talents and temperaments had made them ill suited to the rigours of the bourgeois world, de Nerval wrote: "Ambition was not of our age . . . and the greedy race for position and honours drove us away from spheres of political activity. There remained to us only the poet's ivory tower where we mounted ever higher to isolate ourselves from the crowd. In those high altitudes we breathed at last the pure air of solitude; we drank forgetfulness in the golden cup of legend; we were drunk with poetry and love."

After his death in 1849, at the age of forty, Edgar Allan Poe was likewise absorbed into the bohemian legend of noble failure. In an essay on Poe's life and works, Charles Baudelaire characterised his fate as typical of that awaiting any gifted man compelled to dwell among brutes. Baudelaire cursed the tenor of public opinion in democratic societies such as the United States, warning that no charity or indulgence could be expected from that quarter. Indeed, he asserted, poets "cannot hope to fit in, either in a democratic or an aristocratic society, in a republic or an absolute monarchy. . . . Illustrious unfortunates, [they are] born to suffer the harsh apprenticeship of genius amidst the crowd of mediocre souls."

The moral that Baudelaire drew from Poe's life would become a recurring theme in his poetry, finding its most crystalline expression in the sad flappings of his famous seabird:

The Albatross

Often, to pass the time, sailors
Will catch albatrosses, those great seabirds
Which nonchalantly chaperone ships
Across bitter gulfs.

Hardly have they set them down on the deck
Than these monarchs of the sky, awkward and ashamed,
Piteously let their great white wings
Drag at their sides like pairs of unshipped oars.

How gauche and weak becomes this winged traveller!
How weak and awkward, even comical
He who was but lately so adroit!
One deckhand teases his beak with a branding iron,
Another mimics, by limping, the cripple that once flew!

The Poet is like this sovereign of the clouds,
Riding the storm above the marksman's range;
In exile on earth, hooted and jeered at,
He cannot walk because of his great wings.

In emphasising the dignity and superiority of the rejected ones, bohemia offered a secular counterpart to the Christian account of Jesus' ostracism and crucifixion. Like the Christian pilgrim, the bohemian poet must endure torture at the hands of the uncomprehending masses, but here, just as in the Christian story, such neglect is in itself evidence of the righteousness of the neglected party. Not being understood may be taken as a sign that there is much in one *to* understand. It is because of his massive wings that the poet cannot walk.

5.

The bohemian belief in the inferiority of the group and its traditions had its corollary in a conviction as to the superiority of the individual and the virtue of splitting off from convention.

In 1850, Gérard de Nerval ceased conforming to existing ideas of suitable pets and bought himself a live lobster, which he led around the Jardin du Luxembourg at the end of a blue ribbon. "Why should a lobster be any more ridiculous than a dog," he wondered, "or any other animal that one chooses to take for a walk? I have a liking for lobsters. They are peaceful, serious creatures. They know the secrets of the sea, they don't bark, and they don't gnaw upon one's monadic privacy the way dogs do. Goethe had an aversion to dogs, and he wasn't mad."

Being a great and original artist became synonymous with surprising or, even better, offending the bourgeoisie. On completing *Salammbô* (1862), Flaubert declared that he had written his Carthaginian novel in order to "(1) annoy the bourgeois, (2) unnerve and shock sensitive people, (3) irritate the archaeologists, (4) seem unintelligible to the ladies and (5) earn myself a reputation as a pederast and a cannibal."

In the 1850s, a group of bohemian students in Paris organised a club that they hoped would "offend judges and pharmacists." Having settled on what seemed to them the most effective way of achieving that end, they named themselves the Suicide Club and issued a manifesto avowing that all members would be dead by their own hand by the age of thirty—or before they went bald, whichever came first. Only one actual suicide was reported among the membership, but the club was deemed a success nevertheless after an outraged politician in the Chamber of Deputies delivered a speech branding it an "immoral and illegal monstrosity."

Flaubert's prime ambition for *Salammbô* was scarcely unique: bohemians have always seen it as their special duty to irritate the respectable classes. In New York in 1917, a group of artists who had decided to secede from bourgeois life called for the creation of a "free and independent republic of Greenwich Village," dedicated to art, love, beauty and cigarettes. To mark the birth of their breakaway state, the artists climbed to the top of the Washington Square Arch, drank whiskey, fired cap pistols and read out their own declaration of independence, which consisted simply of the word *whereas,* uttered countless times in rapid succession. Recalling the event many years later, one citizen of the new republic (which lasted until dawn) remarked, "We were radicals devoted to anything—so long as it was taboo in the Mid-West."

Unfortunately for bohemians, the more they have shocked the bourgeoisie, the less willing or able has been the bourgeoisie to be shocked—which has led to an escalating cycle of increasingly extreme antics, as the history of twentieth-century bohemian movements testifies.

"Intelligent man is now a standard type," proposed Dada's founder, Tristan Tzara, in Zurich in 1915, "but the thing we are short of is the *idiotic.* Dada is using all its strength to establish the idiotic everywhere." Thus inspired, Dadaists took to entering smart Zurich restaurants and shouting "Dada" at bourgeois diners. The Dada artist Marcel Duchamp painted a moustache on a copy of the *Mona Lisa* and entitled his work *L.H.O.O.Q.* (*Elle a chaud au cul,* or "She has a hot arse").

For his part, the Dada poet Hugo Ball pioneered a meaningless, multilingual poetry and recited the first example, "Karawane," in a Zurich nightclub, dressed in a suit made out of shiny blue cardboard, with a witch's hat on his head.

Looking back at Dada's goals, the onetime Dadaist painter Hans

Richter remembered, "We wanted to bring forward a new kind of human being, free from the tyranny of rationality, of banality, of generals, fatherlands, nations, art-dealers, microbes, residence permits and the past. To outrage public opinion was our basic principle."

Other groups followed in Dada's footsteps. In 1924, the Surrealists opened the Bureau of Surrealist Enquiries in the rue de Grenelle in Paris. A dress-shop dummy was hung in the window, and members of the public were invited to bring in stories of coincidences and dreams and any new ideas they might have about politics, art or fashion. These were then typed up and tacked on the walls. Antonin Artaud, the director of the bureau, proclaimed, "We need *disturbed* followers far more than we need active followers."

In 1932, no less keen to offend the bourgeoisie, the Italian Futurist Filippo Marinetti published *The Futurist Cookbook,* whose stated purpose was to revolutionise the way Italians ate by weaning them from their nineteenth-century tastes—in particular, their fondness for pasta (the author identified *maccheroni al ragù* and *tagliatelle alla bolognese* as the very epitomes of bourgeois anachronism). But anyone who bought the cookbook hoping for culinary guidance must soon realise that Marinetti was—no less than Gérard de Nerval or Antonin Artaud before him—out to confound expectations. Among the recipes included were

Strawberry Breasts: "A pink plate with two erect feminine breasts made of ricotta dyed pink with Campari and nipples of candied strawberry. Further fresh strawberries under the covering of ricotta make it possible to bite into an ideal multiplication of imaginary breasts."

Aerofood: "Composed of a slice of fennel, an olive and a kumquat, together with a strip of cardboard, on which should be glued, one next to the other, a piece of velvet, a piece of silk, and a piece of sandpaper. The sandpaper is not to be eaten. It is there to be fingered with the right hand while one sucks on the kumquat."

Cubist Vegetable Patch: "1. Little cubes of celery from Verona fried and sprinkled with paprika. 2. Little cubes of fried carrot sprinkled with grated horseradish. 3. Boiled peas. 4. Little pickled onions from Ivrea sprinkled with chopped parsley. 5. Little bars of Fontina cheese. N.B. The cubes must not be larger than one cubic centimetre."

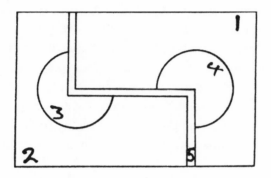

6.

The excesses of bohemia are hardly difficult to discern. It is only a short step from valuing originality and emphasising the nonmaterial aspects of life to feeling that almost anything that could surprise a judge or a pharmacist—from crustacean-walking to strawberry-breast-cooking—must be important.

To cite only one example of excess: so keen have many bohemians been to place spiritual concerns at the forefront of their lives that their indifference to practical affairs has become nearly obsessional. This has on occasion had the paradoxical effect of reducing their existence to an all-consuming struggle merely to survive—leaving them with less time to contemplate matters of the spirit and a greater need to consider problems of the body than even the busiest or most materialistic judge or pharmacist.

In rural Massachusetts, in 1844, a confederacy of utopian-bohemian artists established a communal farm that they named Fruitlands. They flatly stated that they had no interest in money or in work as an end in itself; they wanted only to grow enough to feed themselves so they could turn their energies to more important pursuits—namely, poetry, painting, nature and romantic love. The founder of the community, Bronson Alcott, announced that the mission of the new farmers was "to *be*, not to *do*." He and his fellow members subscribed to a set of ambitious ideals characteristic of bohemian communities both before and after theirs: they wore no cotton clothes (for cotton supported the institution of slavery), consumed no animals or dairy products and kept to a peculiarly strict vegetarian diet, eating only those things that grew high up in the air and shunning carrots and potatoes because they pointed down into the ground, rather than aspiring to Heaven in the manner of apples and pears.

Predictably, the community did not last long. The farmers' reluctance to engage with practicalities forced them, after their first summer at Fruitlands, to wage an urgent battle merely to keep body and soul together—which did not afford them much leisure to read Homer and Petrarch, as they had planned. Emerson, who had met Alcott in Boston a few years before the founding of the farm, recalled of the commune's members, "Their whole doctrine was spiritual, but they always ended up saying, 'Could you please send us some more money?'" Just six months after Fruitlands's high-minded inauguration, the community dispersed in acrimony and despair, adding a new chapter to the familiar bohemian tale of idealism gone sour thanks to an unbending refusal to submit to even minimal bourgeois disciplines.

It would be both senseless and very unusual for anyone to feel anxious over the bourgeois conception of status if this class were truly as misguided and as unimpressive as bohemia is wont to make out. Even granted that many good ideas may be shocking to Midwesterners, it by no means follows that everything that shocks them will be outstanding. It is only because judges and pharmacists do most things extremely well that certain other aspects of their behaviour and mentality come to seem, by contrast, so troublesome—and so tempting to dissent from.

7.

Which is in no way to urge universal restraint in this area. Whatever the excesses of the outer wings of bohemia, the movement's enduring contribution has been to pose a series of well-considered challenges to bourgeois ideology. The bourgeoisie has stood accused of failing to understand the role that wealth should play in a good life; of being too hasty to condemn worldly failure and too slavish in venerating signs of outward success; of placing too much faith in sham notions of propriety; of dogmatically confusing professional qualifications with talent; of neglecting the value of art, sensitivity, playfulness and creativity; and of being overconcerned with order, rules, bureaucracy and timekeeping.

To sum up its significance in the broadest, most comprehensive terms, one might simply suggest that bohemia has legitimised the pursuit of an alternative way of life. It has staked out and defined a subculture in which values that have been consistently underrated or overlooked by the bourgeois mainstream may finally be granted their due authority and prestige.

Like Christianity, for which it has in some sense functioned as an emotional substitute—having first emerged, after all, in the nineteenth century, around the very time when Christianity was beginning to lose its grip on the public imagination—bohemia has articulated a case for a spiritual, as opposed to a material, method of evaluating both oneself and others. Like Christianity's monasteries and nunneries, bohemia's garrets, cafés, low-rent districts and cooperative businesses have provided a refuge where that part of the population which is uninterested in pursuing the bourgeoisie's rewards—money, possessions, status—may find sustenance and fellowship.

Furthermore, the good standing of a number of bohemians past and present has helped to reassure those in doubt—that is, those made most anxious by the dominant status system—that such eccentricity has a long and occasionally distinguished history, stretching from the poets of nineteenth-century Paris to the light-hearted subversives of the Dada movement to the picnicking Surrealists.

A way of life that might in the wrong hands have seemed wayward and absurd has instead, thanks to the most gifted of the bohemians, come to seem serious and laudable. To the role-models of the lawyer, the entrepreneur and the scientist, bohemia has added those of the poet, the traveller and the essayist. It has proposed that these characters, too, whatever their personal oddities and material shortfalls, may be worthy of an elevated status of their own.

8.

A mature solution to status anxiety may be said to begin with the recognition that status is available from, and awarded by, a variety of different audiences—industrialists, bohemians, families, philosophers—and that our choice among them may be free and willed.

However unpleasant anxieties over status may be, it is difficult to imagine a good life entirely free of them, for the fear of failing and disgracing oneself in the eyes of others is an inevitable consequence of harbouring ambitions, of favouring one set of outcomes over another and of having regard for individuals besides oneself. Status anxiety is the price we pay for acknowledging that there is a public distinction between a successful and an unsuccessful life.

Yet if our need for status is a fixed thing, we nevertheless retain all say over where we will fulfil that need. We are at liberty to ensure that our worries about being disgraced will arise principally in relation to an audience whose methods of judgement we both understand and respect. Status anxiety may be defined as problematic only insofar as it is inspired by values that we uphold because we are terrified and preternaturally obedient; because we have been anaesthetized into believing that they are natural, perhaps even God-given; because those around us are in thrall to them; or because we have grown too imaginatively timid to conceive of alternatives.

Philosophy, art, politics, religion and bohemia have never sought to do away entirely with the status hierarchy; they have attempted, rather, to institute new kinds of hierarchies based on sets of values unrecognised by, and critical of, those of the majority. While maintaining a firm grip on the differences between success and failure, good and bad, shameful and honourable, these five entities have endeavoured to remould our sense of what may rightfully be said to belong under those weighty and dichotomous headings.

In so doing, they have helped to lend legitimacy to those who, in every generation, may be unable or unwilling to comply dutifully with the dominant notions of high status, but who may yet deserve to be categorised under something other than the brutal epithet of "loser" or "nobody." They have provided us with persuasive and consoling reminders that there is more than one way—and more than just the judge's and the pharmacist's way—of succeeding at life.

ACKNOWLEDGEMENTS

Special thanks to: Simon Prosser, Caroline Dawnay, Nicole Aragi, Dan Frank, Rahel Lerner, Michael Ledger Lomas, Michael Port, Dominic Houlder, Tom Graves, Felicity Harvey and Austin Taylor.

PICTURE ACKNOWLEDGEMENTS

p. 12   AP Photo; p. 16   Mary Evans Picture Library; p. 18   Stapleton Collection, UK/Bridgeman Art Library; p. 20   The Hoover Company; p. 21   Reprinted by arrangement with Sears, Roebuck and Co. Protected under copyright. No duplication permitted; p. 22–23   GURSKY Andreas Gursky/DACS London 2003, Courtesy Gallery Monika Sprueth, Cologne, 2003; p. 29   Galleria dell'Accademia, Venice/Bridgeman Art Library; p. 48 The British Library, London; p. 49   Corpus Christi College, Oxford/ Bridgeman Art Library; p. 50   Musée Condé, Chantilly/Bridgeman Art Library; p. 70   Bettmann/Corbis; p. 81   Punch Ltd.; p. 136   National Gallery of Art, Washington DC/Bridgeman Art Library; p. 138–9   Ashmolean Museum, Oxford/Bridgeman Art Library; p. 140   National Museum and Gallery of Wales, Cardiff/Bridgeman Art Library; p. 141 Museum Oskar Reinhart am Stadtgarten, Winterthur; p. 142   Kunstindustrimuseet, Copenhagen/photo: Pernille Klemp; p. 144–5   Nivaagaards Malerisamling, Denmark; p. 157   Musée Condé, Chantilly/Bridgeman Art Library; p. 158   Musée de la Ville de Paris, Musée Carnavalet, Paris/ Bridgeman Art Library; p. 160   Louvre, Paris/Bridgeman Art Library; p. 162–3   Courtesy of the Warden and Scholars of New College, Oxford/ Bridgeman Art Library; p. 166   Courtesy of the Warden and Scholars of New College, Oxford/Bridgeman Art Library; p. 167   Punch Ltd.; p. 168t The New Yorker Collection 1995 Peter Steiner from cartoonbank.com. All Rights Reserved; p. 168b   The New Yorker Collection 1987 J. B. Handelsman from cartoonbank.com. All Rights Reserved; p. 169t   The New Yorker Collection 1980 Charles Barsotti from cartoonbank.com. All Rights Reserved; p. 169m   The New Yorker Collection 1988 Bernard Schoenbaum from cartoonbank.com. All Rights Reserved; p. 169b   The New Yorker Collection 1988 Mike Twohy from cartoonbank.com. All Rights Reserved; p. 170   The New Yorker Collection 1998 Michael Crawford from cartoonbank.com. All Rights Reserved; p. 171   The New Yorker Collection 1997 Frank Cotham from cartoonbank.com. All Rights Reserved; p. 172 The New Yorker Collection 1988 William Hamilton from cartoonbank. com. All Rights Reserved; p. 195   Mercedes-Benz/Campbell Doyle Dye; p. 210   Intercontinental Hotels Corporation; p. 211   Agency Merkley/

Newman Harty; p. 212 photo: Alan Mahon/Horton Stephens photographer's agents; p. 226 Musée de Tesse, Le Mans/Bridgeman Art Library; p. 227 Private Collection/Lauros/Giraudon/Bridgeman Art Library; p. 231 Louvre, Paris/Bridgeman Art Library; p. 232–3 Courtesy of the Trustees of Sir John Soane's Museum, London/Bridgeman Art Library; p. 236 Stapleton Collection, UK/Bridgeman Art Library; p. 237 Stapleton Collection, UK/Bridgeman Art Library; p. 240–241 Corcoran Gallery of Art, Washington, DC; p. 242–3 Bolton Museum & Art Gallery, Lancashire, England; p. 244–5 The Collection of the Newark Museum, Newark, NJ. Purchase 1961 The Members' Fund, 61.516; p. 259 Lauros/Giraudon/Bridgeman Art Library; p. 260 London Aerial Photo Library/Corbis; p. 262–3 Architectural Association Photo Library/Mary Parsons; p. 266 Lee Miller Archives, Chiddingly, England; p. 271 Louvre, Paris/Bridgeman Art Library; p. 272 Musée Fabre, Montpellier/Bridgeman Art Library; p. 278 Lee Miller Archives, Chiddingly, England; p. 280–81 Yale Center for British Art, Paul Mellon Collection, USA/Bridgeman Art Library; p. 286 Galleria Pictogramma, Rome/Bridgeman Art Library/Alinari.

INDEX

Page numbers in *italics* refer to illustrations.